ALTARATION
THE MYSTERY OF THE MASS REVEALED

Student Workbook

Mark Hart

ASCENSION PRESS

West Chester, Pennsylvania

Nihil obstat: Rev. Msgr. Joseph G. Prior, S.S.L., S.T.D.
                  Censor Librorum
                  February 18, 2015

Imprimatur: +Most Reverend Charles J. Chaput, O.F.M. Cap.
                  Archbishop of Philadelphia
                  February 22, 2015

Ascension Press
Post Office Box 1990
West Chester, PA 19380
1-800-376-0520
AscensionPress.com

Cover Design: Devin Schadt

Printed in the United States of America

ISBN: 978-1-935940-73-9

Contents

THE 5 MOST IMPORTANT THINGS IN MY LIFE ...

1 _____

2 _____

3 _____

4 _____

5 _____

THE 5 THINGS THAT TAKE UP THE MOST TIME IN MY LIFE ...

1
_____

2
_____

3
_____

4
_____

5
_____

Dear Friend,

People camp out all night for tickets to movie premieres, concerts, and playoff games. They stand in the pouring rain and biting cold for hours to see their favorite band or cheer on the home team. Others stay up all night after gorging themselves on Thanksgiving dinner to be first in line when the stores open on Black Friday. They do these things because they are passionate about the things they love and adore the most.

What about you? Have you ever done anything like this? What is most important in your life?

Consider your Instagram or Twitter feed. What do they say about you and where your attention goes? What do you think about more than anything else? What do you treasure most in this world? What things and people occupy most of your time and energy?

If God or the Catholic Faith are not first on your list, or even in the top three, is it any wonder why you find Mass so boring, outdated, or "optional"? If you do not have a relationship with God—or even have the desire to have a relationship with him—then of course Mass is not going to make your to-do list.

If this sounds a bit like you, I understand where you are. I have been there. I have struggled with finding Mass boring and wondered, "What's the point?" But I have come to realize there is much more than meets the eye when it comes to everything about God, including Mass. This is why I wanted to create this program. It is my prayer that, as you enter into this journey with me, you will discover why you are here, why God created you, and what he created you for. I hope that you will discover the purpose, mission, and plan of your life—and, in the process, that you will come to see that there is a lot more going on at Mass than you ever imagined.

Over the course of this program, you will probably discover a few things that will surprise you. You will come to see and hear things that you have experienced hundreds of times in a totally new light. For the first time, they will actually make sense. By the end of this program, I guarantee that you will come to see Mass is anything but boring. In fact, if you truly enter into it, I promise that you will come to understand how the great mystery that is the Mass is incredibly relevant to your life.

Thank you for opening your heart, turning the page, and taking the journey.

All for Jesus,

Mark Hart

Every time I say the Mass, the universe is changed.

— FR. MIKE SCHMITZ —

More Than the Eye

"The LORD sees not as man sees; man looks on the outward appearance, but the LORD looks on the heart."

– 1 Samuel 16:7

Lord God, you remind us in these words from the Bible that things are not always as they seem to be on the surface. For just as we are more than our outward appearance, so is the Mass. Thank you for the gift of the Mass, even if we don't yet completely understand it. Please be with us during this journey. Open our eyes and ears and hearts to all that you want to reveal to us.

We ask this through Christ our Lord.

Amen.

DIVE IN

If I said, "The Lord be with you," what would be your natural reply?

"And with your spirit," right? (Or, if you haven't been to Mass much over the past few years, "... and also with you.")

"... when we enter into the Mass, we are no longer functioning on an earthly level."

It is a "programmed" response for Catholics, offered as automatically as "God bless you" when someone sneezes. But is it meant to be more than that? How much of what we do at Mass is just a habit?

Every time you enter a church for Mass, you bless yourself with holy water. In those moments, how often do you consider the gift of your baptism? You then proceed to a pew and genuflect prior to entering. Is it humility and reverence or just habit that drives you to your knee? Why only one knee and not both? In the Liturgy of the Word, we sit for the First and Second readings but stand for the Gospel. Why? We kneel during the Eucharistic Prayer but stand for the Our Father. Is there a point to all these "ups and downs" or is the Church putting us through a low-impact cardio workout?

What about the language used by the priest? Is there anywhere else in your life that you "partake," invite someone to "enter under your roof,"
or ponder God's "serene and kindly countenance"? How often do you feel "imbued with heavenly mysteries"? Why doesn't the Church just "dumb down" the language a little and "get with the times"? Why don't the pope and the bishops speak our language? Why does the Church insist on speaking its own way?

In a nutshell, when we enter into the Mass, we are no longer functioning on an earthly level. The Church uses "heavenly" language in the Mass because it is set apart from earthly realities. The Mass really isn't about Jesus coming to earth as much as it is God lifting us up into heaven for an hour.

It is for this reason that we need to move through the natural human distractions and really try to "lean in" to the Mass. Moving beyond what is on the surface, we will begin to respond rather than react. We will soon discover that there is so much more to the Mass than meets the eye.

DISCUSSION QUESTIONS

Segment 1: I Was Bored, Too

What do you hope to get out of this program on the Mass?

_____

_____

_____

_____

Were you surprised to hear the author and presenter of a program on the Mass tell you how bored he was at Mass as a kid?

_____

_____

_____

_____

Most of us have been bored at Mass. Why do you think that is?

_____

_____

_____

_____

Why does God desire our sacrifice? What does sacrifice teach us?

_____

_____

_____

_____

Segment 2: I Will Follow

Did it surprise you to discover that the two men are priests? What do you think of them?

_____

_____

_____

Do you tend to see priests as normal men with the same struggles as everyone else, or do you see them as different somehow?

_____

_____

_____

Why was Fr. Josh surprised to hear God say, "I love you," when he asked him what he wanted him to do? Do you think you need to "earn" God's love?

_____

_____

_____

Fr. Mike talks about the importance of a priest acting as a father to his people. How is the priest's role as a spiritual father similar to that of a "regular" father?

_____

_____

_____

Segment 3: The Power of the Priesthood

Why is the Catholic priesthood unique?

_____

_____

_____

What does the phrase _in persona Christi_ mean to a priest's daily ministry? Have you ever thought of the priest as "another Christ"?

_____

_____

_____

Has your view of the priesthood changed at all as a result of this presentation?

_____

_____

_____

ENTERING THE MYSTERY

Parents are supposed to live forever ... at least, that is what you think when you are a child.

I will never forget the first time it really hit me that my parents would die one day. I was just out of college and working in my first full-time job. When the phone rang that random Thursday afternoon, little did I know how much my life would change forever.

It was my father on the line. "Your mom's in the hospital, son. Her blood pressure is dropping and they need to get her in for surgery right away. It's not looking good. Get here as soon as you can," he said, as he choked back emotions he wasn't comfortable showing.

When I arrived at the hospital, I found my father and two of my older brothers talking to a doctor. The floor and walls were sterile and cold, but the conversation was quite intense. Apparently, my mother needed immediate surgery, and time was ticking away. "We need to go now, Mr. Hart," the doctor said to my father in an urgent tone. I will never forget seeing my mother as they wheeled her out. She was visibly uncomfortable, holding her rosary in one hand and reaching for my father's hand with the other.

It was at that moment that one of my older brothers— the one who had decided he no longer believed in God and wanted nothing to do with Church—looked at me and mockingly asked, "So where's your God now?"

I had never felt angrier yet at the same time more filled with pity for another person in my whole life. There was my brother, seeking a God whom he had abandoned but who would never abandon him. I replied, "God is expecting me to pray. So why don't you join me and get his attention?" So my brother and I went to the hospital chapel. We fell on our knees on the cold linoleum tile and asked God to heal our mother if it was his will.

My mother's surgery was successful, and she was showing signs of progress. Two days later, though, there were complications, and she needed another operation. Eventually, she was released from the hospital, fragile but healing. Two days after she returned home, I went to help out. I found my saintly mother on the couch, visibly uncomfortable but smiling nonetheless. Upon entering the kitchen, I was reminded that my father's talents, though vast, did not extend to cooking. Dirty dishes had piled up. Trash was overflowing. A used skillet sat upon the stove marked with the visible residue of a culinary experiment gone terribly wrong.

I grabbed the overstuffed garbage bag to take it outside, only to have the red plastic handle snap in my hand from the bag's immense weight. Finally, pulling it all together, I walked from the kitchen through the living room where my mother "rested" looking like a sanitation engineer version of Santa with my bag of trash and takeout containers.

Seeing me, my mom exclaimed, "Mark, honey, you better call the priest." I stopped dead in my tracks. Dropping the trash bag, I rushed to the couch. "What is it, Mom? Are you OK? Can you see Grandma?" (This was a stupid thing to say to a loved one you fear might be dying.)

"No, I'm fine," she said. With a grin, she added, "It's just that in over twenty years I've never seen you take out the trash without being asked." Laughing at how she had gotten me, I took out the trash. As I took off the lid of the garbage can and dropped in the bag, it hit me. I wasn't a child of God as much as I was a *brat* of God.

For twenty-two years I had taken out the trash because I was told to. Rarely, if ever, did I do so out of love for my parents. It was then that the Holy Spirit launched a full-scale attack on my soul, dropping bombs of grace-filled understanding on me.

How many Sundays and holy days had I gone to Mass not because I loved God but because I was told to go? How many times had I prayed to God to get me out of a jam instead of to become holy? How many confessions had I made in the hope of avoiding hell but not because I really desired heaven?

What about you? Do you go to Mass because you are forced to go or to get to know God better on a personal level? Do you go to Mass for what you "get" or to give something? Is your faith as a Catholic based on rules or on a relationship with God? *Altaration* is designed to help you take a fresh, deeper look at Mass. It isn't just about what you *get* from Mass but what you *bring* to it.

Love doesn't wait for the phone call to start caring ... love pursues. God is love. He is inviting you to love him. He has been pursuing you because he wants you to have a personal relationship with him. The Mass is where you can let God "catch" you. Forget what you think you know about the Mass, and be open to letting it transform your mind and illuminate your soul.

How far are you willing to go for the One who loves you? How well you enter into this study is your answer.

CHALLENGE

of the week

- [ ] Say a prayer for your parish priests every night before you go to bed. Mention them to God by name.

- [ ] After Sunday Mass, take a minute to thank the priest for offering Mass and tell him something you appreciated from his homily.

Share your experience here:

_____

_____

_____

_____

_____

_____

_____

_____

_____

_____

_____

_____

_____

WRAP-UP

Priests like Fr. Mike and Fr. Josh have not just decided to be Catholic but to give their very lives to serve the Church. More specifically, they have given their lives to *you*. They now live as "other Christs," fully embracing God's call and serving his people every day. Once they realized the gift of the Eucharist, everything changed. It was clear there was only one vocation that would truly make them happy.

While not everyone is called to be a priest, God's grace comes to us through the sacraments of the Church, especially the Eucharist. The very fuel we need to live a happy and fulfilled life is found on the altar at every Mass.

Things are not always what they seem. This is especially true with the Mass. At one time or another, we may have found Mass to be boring or irrelevant to our lives, but once we understand that Mass is not meant to entertain us, we can appreciate the richness and beauty that lies before us. This is exactly what we will be doing over the next few weeks.

Closing Prayer

"I will put my law within them, and I will write it upon their hearts; and I will be their God, and they shall be my people."

– Jeremiah 31:33

Lord God, thank you for the priesthood. Thank you for loving us enough to call these men to serve us, your people, by celebrating the sacraments, especially the Eucharist. Thank you for reminding us that you not only want to love us from heaven but to be with us on earth. Help us to be more attentive at Mass, to focus more on what you are saying to us through your Word, your priests, and your Eucharist. Please bless our Church, our pope, our bishops, and our priests. We ask this through Christ our Lord. Amen.

FIND IT

Early Christians in Rome, threatened with death for practicing their faith, celebrated Mass in the catacombs. What are the catacombs? Why were they considered "safe"?

Any Questions?

Why do we have to go to Mass?

God doesn't have to love us as a Father; he freely chooses to do so. Nor did he "have to" give us his only Son to die for our sins and grant us the possibility of eternal life. God's creativity is outdone only by his generosity.

So rather than asking why we should go to Mass, here is the question we should be asking: "Is God worth it?" Is taking one hour a week to worship the God who has blessed us with everything we have worth it? Is having an hour set aside to let God love us while we try to love him worth it? Do we think created things are more important than the One who created them?

Everything we have is a gift from God—every blessing in our lives, every person, talent, ability, and interest—every good gift. The Mass is the greatest gift God gives us. When we come to be more aware of our own sins and our need for a savior, the more clearly we see the Mass as not merely an obligation but an opportunity not to be missed.

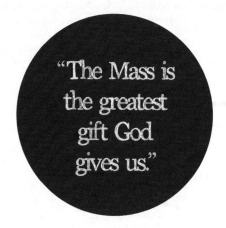

"The Mass is the greatest gift God gives us."

Why is the priesthood so important?

In a nutshell, because without the priesthood, there would be no Mass, no celebration of the Eucharist.

The role of priests in the Old Testament was simple: They were God's representatives to his people, offering sacrifices on behalf of the people in atonement for their sins.

Jesus established a "New Covenant," a new, binding relationship between God and his people, the Church. This New Covenant has a new priesthood, one that shares in the authority of Christ the High Priest. The priests of the Church, then, bring God to us—and us to God—through their teaching and ministry (particularly the sacraments). They act *in persona Christi* ("in the person of Christ"), with Jesus' own authority

and power, given to them in their ordination. They are his hands, feet, and voice on earth; they are the instruments God uses to carry out his saving ministry to his people.

Think of it this way: The Catholic priesthood is the continuation of Jesus' healing, teaching, and feeding since his ascension. It is Jesus' way of keeping his love and mercy "real" and personal in every generation. In his priests, Jesus is borrowing other men's hands, eyes, and voices to deliver his Body and Blood to each living soul in every generation for their freedom and eternal life. A priest sins and has the same struggles as the rest of us, but he uniquely brings Christ to the world through his ministry.

WHAT'S THAT WORD?

GENUFLECTION

Prior to entering or exiting a pew, we *genuflect* (from the Latin *genuflectere* for "to bend one's knee"), kneeling down on one knee as an outward sign of our interior reverence for the presence of Christ in the Eucharist, which is reserved in the tabernacle.

Kneeling is a profound symbol of adoration, falling on our knees before the King of the universe. Throughout Scripture, we see heroes and heroines falling prostrate to worship God, as the Magi did in Bethlehem before the infant Jesus (see Matthew 2:11) or Christ's disciples did in Simon Peter's boat following a mighty storm at sea (see Matthew 14:33).

SANCTUARY

From a Latin word for "sacred" or "holy place," the "sanctuary" is the area of a church, where liturgical actions take place. Usually elevated by steps and located at the front or center of the church, the "sanctuary" contains the altar, the tabernacle, the *ambo* (where the readings are proclaimed and the homily is given by the priest or deacon), the credence table, and the presider's chair (where the priest celebrant sits). The sanctuary is set apart and entered only by those who are ministers for the Mass, such as the priest, deacon, altar servers, reader, cantor, and extraordinary ministers. It is appropriate to bow to the altar when entering the sanctuary to acknowledge the sacredness of the space. If, as in many churches, the tabernacle is present within the sanctuary, it is appropriate to genuflect as well. Though church sanctuaries have different architectural designs, the sanctuary is a holy space that deserves our highest reverence.

AND WITH YOUR SPIRIT.

Right back at ya.
You got it.
Peace.
You, too.

I am sure all of you have had a conversation with someone where they say something and you immediately reply—where you throw back a comment or answer a question without really thinking about it. You might fall into the same routine during Mass, responding without thinking. When the priest says, "The Lord be with you," why do we respond, "And with your spirit"?

There are a number of reasons, actually.

In the Mass, the priest acts not as an individual Christian, but in the place of Christ himself: He acts *in persona Christi* (Latin for "in the person of Christ"). So we are not just greeting the celebrant, akin to saying, "Right back at ya, Father." We are acknowledging the very essence of who he is—the one standing in the person of Christ leading us in the "source and summit" of the Church's life, the Mass (see CCC 1324–1327).

This formal greeting acknowledges the very core of the person—his spirit. When St. Paul wrote to Timothy, he addressed his "spirit" (see 2 Timothy 4:22). Hippolytus, writing in the year 215, noted that Christians offered greetings to the "spirit" of a priest. As we say the words, "and with your Spirit," we pray for the priest, that he might continue to live his priesthood with faith and enthusiasm for God's people.

GOD SHOWED US, IN THE FLESH, WHAT

LOVE

LOOKS LIKE.

Mark Hart

Our Father's Plan

"For God so loved the world that he gave his only Son, that whoever believes in him should not perish but have eternal life."

– John 3:16

Heavenly Father, thank you for this opportunity to learn more about you and about your plan of salvation. Help us to begin to understand how much you love us and to grow in understanding and in gratitude. Thank you for sending your Son to save us by taking on our sins and by dying and rising again so that we may have life. Send your Spirit upon us now to enlighten us and to guide us.

We ask this through Christ our Lord.

Amen.

DIVE IN

I once heard the following story told by Paul Harvey, one of the most popular radio hosts of the twentieth century. This is one of those stories that takes a complex reality and makes it simple, much like Jesus did through his parables. Mr. Harvey told it this way:

There was a kind, decent, mostly good man, generous to his family, upright in his dealings with other men. But he just didn't believe all that Incarnation stuff that the churches proclaim at Christmastime. He just couldn't swallow the "Jesus Story," about God coming to earth as a man. "I'm not going with you to church this Christmas Eve," he told his wife, stating that he would feel like a hypocrite. And so he stayed, and his family went to the midnight service.

Shortly after the family drove away, snow began to fall. He watched the flurries getting heavier and then went back to his fireside chair to read his newspaper. Minutes later, he was startled by a thudding sound ... then another. Sort of a thump. At first, he thought someone must be throwing snowballs against his living room window. But when he went to the front door to investigate, he found a flock of birds huddled miserably in the snow. They had been caught in the storm and, in

"The man finally came to see what Christmas is all about."

a desperate search for shelter, had tried to fly through his large landscape window. Well, he couldn't let the poor creatures lie there and freeze, so he remembered the barn where his children stabled their pony. That would provide a warm shelter if he could direct the birds to it.

Quickly, he put on a coat and tramped through the deepening snow to the barn. He opened the doors wide and turned on a light, but the birds did not come in. So he hurried back to the house, fetched breadcrumbs, and sprinkled them on the snow, making a trail to the yellow-lighted, wide-open doorway of the stable. But to his dismay, the birds ignored the breadcrumbs and continued to flap around helplessly in the snow. He tried catching them ... He tried shooing them into the barn by walking around them waving his arms ... Instead, they scattered in every direction, except into the warm, lighted barn. And then he realized they were afraid of him. To them, he reasoned, I am a strange and terrifying creature.

If only I could think of some way to let them know that they can trust me ... that I am not trying to hurt them, but to help them. But how? Any move he made tended to frighten them, confuse them.

They just would not follow. They would not be led because they feared him. If only I could be a bird, he thought, and mingle with them and speak their language. Then I could tell them not to be afraid. Then I could show them the way to the safe, warm barn. But I would have to be one of them so they could see and hear and understand.

At that moment, the church bells began to ring. He stood there listening to the bells playing "Adeste Fidelis" and pealing the glad tidings of Christmas. And he sank to his knees in the snow.

The man finally came to see what Christmas is all about. In the birds in his barn, he came to see why God needed to become man to save us. Jesus, the God-Man, was born as a baby so he could be truly one with humanity. (The Hebrew name *Yeshua*, which is "Jesus" in Greek, literally means "God saves.") God comes to us where *we are* to guide us to where *he is*, so that we can spend eternity with him in heaven. The same is true in every single Mass: In the Eucharist, God comes to us—to save us and to guide us back to himself so that we might be with him forever.

DISCUSSION QUESTIONS

Segment 1: The Incarnation

Jesus was the only founder of a major world religion to claim to be God. What does that mean to you?

It means to me that he is thy only God

God became man in the Incarnation. The Second Person of the Trinity willingly came down from heaven to become "one of us" in everything but sin. What do you think this says about God?

It says that he cares about us.

In the video, Mark Hart says, "God came to show us what Love is." Discuss what you think he means.

I think he means that he is going to teach us.

Have you ever sacrificed something special for another person or had someone sacrifice something for you? How did this impact your relationship with him or her?

This impacted me by becoming friends with people.

Segment 2: A Father Who Loves Us

You heard that some young people around the world are willing to risk their lives to go to Mass. What does that tell you about the value they place on their faith?

It tells me that they really care.

The rules your parents have in place flow from their love for you. What about God's rules or commandments? What do you think a society without rules would look like?

I think that it'll be choas.

Chris says that if God is at the center of our lives, everything else will fall into its proper place. Have you made something else (e.g., sports, music, friends, the Internet) the center of your life rather than God?

No

Segment 3: Priorities

What is the craziest thing you have ever done for something you valued? Was it worth it?

I'm not sure

How can we hear God if we are always plugged into some type of media? Do you ever take time to turn off the "noise" and enjoy the silence?

When it's getting close to night time

Do you value your time with God, even above other things? If not, how would your life change if you did?

It would change by thinking differently.

ENTERING THE MYSTERY

"He was incarnate of the Virgin Mary and became man."

As Christians, we acknowledge the birth of Jesus each year on Christmas. But there is something more at work here, a much deeper truth.

Nine months before Christmas, on March 25th, the Church celebrates the Annunciation of the Lord, when Mary's "yes" to the words of the archangel Gabriel made her the mother of Jesus and the Mother of God (see Luke 1:38). From that moment, we believe that the Second Person of the Trinity, the Son of God, "was incarnate" in Mary's womb.

As an eternal divine Person, the Son of God has always existed. He is "consubstantial" with (i.e., a philosophical term meaning "of the same substance as") God the Father. At a specific moment in history, just over two thousand years ago, he took on a true human nature and was born of Mary. He became like us in everything but sin. When he took on our flesh, Jesus also took on our sufferings (see Hebrews 5:7).

So why did God become man? Why did the "Word become flesh"?

The Nicene Creed, which we pray every Sunday at Mass, gives us the answer: "Through him [Jesus] all things were made. For us men and for *our salvation*, he came down from heaven" (emphasis added).

The eternal Son of God, then, came down from heaven and became man to *save us*. Save us from what? From our sins, so that we can live a life in friendship with God on earth and have a relationship with him in heaven forever.

St. Paul, in his letter to the Philippians, explains it this way:

> Christ Jesus, who, though he was in the form of God, did not count equality with God a thing to be grasped, but emptied himself, taking the form of a servant, being born in the likeness of men. And being found in human form he humbled himself and became obedient unto death, even death on a Cross (Philippians 2:5-8).

These words contain very deep truths. God took on flesh, a real human nature. Through the Incarnation, God "meets us where we are at," walking and pointing us to where we need to go. As you pray the Nicene Creed every Sunday at Mass, take special note of the section proclaiming the Incarnation of Christ. Notice that it highlights Jesus' eternal nature: Even though he was born at a certain point in history, he has always been. He became what we are to give us a share in what he is: divine. He came down to us to "bring us up" to him.

CHALLENGE

of the week

☐ Read the four assigned readings for this Sunday's Mass in advance. As with every Sunday and holy day, there are four readings: the First Reading (usually from the Old Testament), the Responsorial Psalm, the Second Reading (often from one of St. Paul's letters), and the Gospel. (There are many excellent online versions as well as printed missals.)

☐ Write some personal intentions to pray during Mass this Sunday. If your mind wanders during Mass, you can read what you have written and bring them to the Lord.

Share your experience here:

_____
_____
_____
_____
_____
_____
_____
_____
_____
_____
_____
_____
_____

WRAP-UP

Do you believe that you have a Father in heaven who wants nothing but what is best for you? The Bible is full of examples of God acting for the good of his people throughout the course of human history. The clearest example of this is Jesus Christ. Fully God, fully man, he came down from heaven and became incarnate of the Virgin Mary to save us from our sins.

The *Catechism of the Catholic Church* (CCC), which contains the core teachings of the Catholic Faith, says that God "tirelessly calls" each one of us to him (CCC 2567). As Chris Stefanick points out in the video, God wants what is best for is, so he gave us the commandments to help us live free, happy, and joyful lives. He gives us all the graces and gifts necessary for our salvation, but we have a part to play. We need to dispose ourselves properly to hear him and meet him in the sacraments, especially in the Eucharist.

Some Catholics make the mistake of viewing Mass strictly through the lens of what they "get" from it. While we do "get" to hear God's Word proclaimed and receive the Body and Blood of Christ at every Mass, we should also ask ourselves, "What am I bringing to Mass?"

What do you bring to Mass? Praise and prayers? Distraction and boredom? As Jesus tells us, "Ask, and it will be given you; seek, and you will find; knock, and it will be opened to you" (Matthew 7:7). Notice how each of these three actions—asking, seeking, and knocking—require some effort on our part. If you are truly seeking God at Mass—or anywhere else for that matter—you have to put in some effort to connect with him. Once your heart moves toward God, you will come to realize that you aren't actually pursuing him as much as he is pursuing you.

As we move onto the next session, be prepared to open your eyes and your hearts to a deeper reality of what God has done for you ... and what he has in store for you at Mass.

Closing Prayer

"The life I now live in the flesh I live by faith in the Son of God, who loved me and gave himself for me."

– Galatians 2:20

Lord Jesus, sometimes we think we have it all figured out, but, really, we are lost without you. Thank you for loving us enough to die for us. Thank you for wanting so much for us that you gave us the commandments, the Church, and the Mass. Help us to understand how to die to our own bad habits and selfishness so that we can live for you. Help us, like St. Paul, to understand that we are not our own, but that we are yours and that you live within us. Amen.

Any Questions?

How can Jesus be fully God and fully man?

As Clark Kent, Superman looked and dressed like an ordinary guy. He "disguised" his superhero nature through his exterior appearance. Bruce Wayne, on the other hand, was really just an ordinary man without any superpowers. When he put on his Batman suit, though, he appeared to be something more than he really was. He became Batman.

Jesus isn't like either of these fictional characters. On the one hand, Jesus is not like Superman, who tried to look and act like a normal human being but really was not. Jesus is completely human; he is a "true man." He did not come wearing a "disguise." On the other hand, Jesus is not like Batman, who just acted like he was superhuman, performing amazing feats beyond the normal man. Jesus is always "true God," a divine Person.

In the first few centuries of Christianity, this truth about Jesus being both fully human and fully divine was heavily debated, with many arguing heretically that he was either human *or* divine, or that he was "half human and half divine." The truth of the hypostatic union—the unique reality that Jesus was both fully human and fully divine—was clarified by the Church as time went on, most specifically at the Councils of Nicaea in AD 325, Ephesus in 431, and Chalcedon in 451.

> "Put simply: God became like us so we can become like him."

Jesus was "like his brethren in every respect" except sin (see Hebrews 2:17, 4:15). So Jesus got stomachaches and headaches. Jesus could get sunburned and parched in the heat. He sneezed. He laughed (see Psalm 2:4), and he wept (see John 11:35). He is completely human, just like you and me—but without sin. Remember, though, that he is a divine Person, with a human nature and a divine nature. He walked on water, raised the dead, multiplied loaves, and cleansed the lepers. In this sense, while on earth, he was capable of performing miracles—and forgiving sins— because he is God.

The reality of Jesus' human and divine natures is reflected throughout the New Testament. Check out the following verses: Mark 8:31, 9:31, 10:33-34, 13:32, 14:18-20, 26-30; Acts 1:7.

In several ways, the Church mirrors the hypostatic union of Jesus. The Church, founded by Christ and guided by the Holy Spirit, is divine in its origin and nature. At the same time, the Church is made up of sinners and is also completely human (see Romans 12:4; 1 Corinthians 12:12; and 1 Peter 2:5).

Put simply: God became like us so we can become like him.

Can we trust God to provide for our needs?

Throughout salvation history, God has always met the needs of his people. In the Old Testament, the book of Numbers describes how the Israelites, God's Chosen People, wandered in the desert for forty years after their exodus from slavery in Egypt. This wandering was a result of their rebellion against God. But during that long, difficult period, they never went hungry. God fed them with manna, "bread from heaven" (see Numbers 11:1-9). Even in their sinfulness, God showed them his loving care for them.

Remember the Gospel story about the hungry masses of people on the side of the Sea of Galilee and the boy with only a few loaves and fish? When Jesus was finished, they all had full stomachs, with bread and fish to spare. What about the entire human race, dead in sin before Christ's victorious and heroic death on the Cross? God does not just give us the bare minimum; he exceeds our needs—every day.

How did the early Christians go from the idea of "manna" to understanding Jesus as the true "Bread from heaven"? How did the apostles go from hearing they would need to eat Jesus' flesh to actually worshiping the Eucharist as God's own Body?

The New Testament offers tangible examples of how the "culture" of worship of God's people changed. The most significant change was the shift of communal worship from the seventh day, Saturday—the traditional Sabbath of God's people—to the first day of the week, Sunday—to commemorate Jesus' resurrection (see Acts 2:42, 20:7; 1 Corinthians 16:2).

Almost overnight, the early disciples, nearly all of whom were Jews, abandoned celebrating the Sabbath on Saturday. In addition, the way they worshiped brought a new fulfillment to age-old prayers and rituals. The apostles, having received the commission by Jesus to "make disciples of all nations" (Matthew 28:19), assumed the role of leadership in the Church's worship, and the Eucharist was the heart of the Liturgy from the first days of the Church: "And they devoted themselves to the apostles' teaching and fellowship, to the breaking of bread and the prayers" (Acts 2:42).

God's plan from the very beginning was to fill us with his own divine life. But it was difficult even for Jesus' followers to understand and accept the truth of his words: "Truly, truly, I say to you, unless you eat the flesh of the Son of man and drink his blood, you have no life in you" (John 6:53; see also John 6:25-68). In the Eucharist, Jesus gives us a share in his own divine life. This is why, as Catholics, our lives, prayer, and worship are all centered around the Eucharist, "the source and summit" of our faith (CCC 1324). Everything we are and do flows from the altar and back toward it.

Evidence for the Church's belief in the real presence of Christ in the Eucharist can be found in the writings of St. Paul: "The cup of blessing which we bless, is it not a *participation in the blood of Christ*? The bread which we break, is it not a *participation in the body of Christ*?" (1 Corinthians 10:16, emphasis added).

St. Paul was not the only apostolic writer who taught that the Eucharist is the literal Body and Blood of Christ. As St. Peter, the first pope, writes: "[Jesus] has granted to us his precious and very great promises, that through these you may escape from the corruption that is in the world because of

"Our Father in heaven gives us our daily bread ..."

passion, and become *partakers of the divine nature*" (2 Peter 1:4, emphasis added).

We always need to remember that when we receive the Eucharist, we are not just eating bread or drinking wine. As Jesus himself taught, we are eating his very Body and Blood. So when we receive our Eucharistic Lord in Communion, we are "abiding" in him and he in us in the most tangible way possible (see John 15:4-6; 1 John 2:27-28, 4:13). We are united with him, Body, Blood, Soul, and Divinity.

When we seek the Eucharist, hunger for it, and attend Mass and Adoration often, we have Christ literally at the center of our physical lives. Our Father in heaven gives us our daily bread; he fulfills us in a way nothing else can, and his deepest hope for us is that we would go to him daily to have our deepest hunger satisfied.

WHAT'S THAT WORD?

PREFACE

You might not recognize the name "preface," but when you hear the words that follow, you will recognize the moment within the Mass. (The following "conversation" between the priest and the people is actually called the "Preface Dialogue," which is only the first part of the Preface of the Mass.)

Priest: **The Lord be with you.**
People: **And with your spirit.**
Priest: **Lift up your hearts.**
People: **We lift them up to the Lord.**
Priest: **Let us give thanks to the Lord our God.**
People: **It is right and just.**

You have heard and responded to these words hundreds of times at Mass. How often, though, do you really think about what you are saying? The priest is praying that God's spirit might be alive and active within you ("The Lord be with you")—and you return the prayer ("And with your spirit"). Why? Because both you and the priest are going to need the power of the Holy Spirit to handle what is about to happen.

So what exactly is about to happen?

You are about to lay your life, hopes, dreams, fears, anxieties—your very self—upon the altar, to be consumed and transformed by the God of the universe.

Go ahead and read that sentence again. It is dense.

We cannot be dense, however, to the magnitude of what we are praying at this moment of the Mass. We are not simply giving a rote response; we are giving God permission to take, break, and remake our lives in him. Think hard about this moment and whether or not

you mean what you are saying. Do you give God permission to give you a "spiritual heart transplant"? Are you willing to forsake "false gods" (e.g., friends who are a bad influence, gossip, overuse of social media and technology ... and the list goes on) for him? And are you grateful to God for his personal love for you as his unique, "unrepeatable" creation? You ought to be. It surely is "right and just" to give thanks to God, the Author of Life, to give him your full and undivided attention, both during the Mass and in your daily life

Of course, there are many other moments and ways we turn our attention to God. For example, the way you choose to participate (or not participate) during Mass determines how attentive you will be to what is going on. Do you dress appropriately and act reverently? Do you join in singing the hymns as best you can? Do you say the responses deliberately and thoughtfully? Do you listen to the readings and homily with your mind and heart engaged? The more we realize that the Mass is about what Jesus did for us and our relationship with him, the more we realize that how we dress, act, and participate can either draw us (and others) closer to him or pull us away.

Before Mass, ask the Holy Spirit to give you eyes for heaven, to free you from the visible desires of this life and prepare you for the endless happiness of the next. As you grow in understanding of the earthly and the heavenly elements of the Mass, you will more fully trust in what you cannot see—spiritual, heavenly realities—and grow in gratitude for what you can see—the blessings you have received here on earth.

PENITENTIAL ACT

Have you ever been in a conversation and sensed some tension? Maybe you said something you shouldn't have or did something in the past that hurt or offended another person. Unless you want the uncomfortable feeling to continue, you realize that you need to say something to clear the air—apologize maybe—so you can move past the issue. In a similar way, this is the case when we approach God in prayer at the beginning of Mass.

When we arrive at church for Mass, we can be burdened with things we have done during the previous week, sins committed against God or against others. These can cause distance or tension between God and us. So, at the beginning of the Mass, we acknowledge our need to set things right with God so that we will be able to offer the highest form of prayer to him. But we do more than just "clear the air"; we announce our faults and our need for forgiveness in the Penitential Act. (To be "penitential" means to be sincerely sorry for our sins, and a "rite" is a solemn ceremonial action.)

The Penitential Act (also known as the "Penitential Rite") has three forms. The longest form includes the *Confiteor,* which begins, "I confess to Almighty God, and to you my brothers and sisters ..." You probably recognize the prayer. In it, we confess that we are sinners, acknowledging that we are at fault for our sins in the part known as the *Mea Culpa:* "Through my fault, through my fault, through my most grievous fault" (in Latin, *"Mea culpa, mea culpa, mea maxima culpa"*).

Whenever we pray these words, we should seek to call to mind anything we have done that has offended God or hurt others. The Church not only asks us to admit our "most grievous fault" but also that we demonstrate our need for repentance by striking our chests three times as we say the words. By doing this, we associate a physical action with our words to give our worship a fuller meaning. We are not "beating ourselves up" about it, but showing ourselves—and one another—that repentance involves our entire person, soul *and* body.

In praying the *Mea Culpa,* the Church invites us to realize that if we are going to say we are sorry, we need to really mean it. We are actually doing more than merely saying that we are sorry for our sins and asking God for his forgiveness: We are admitting that it is *our fault,* and that we need God's grace and the prayers of our community to avoid sinning again.

At the end of the Penitential Act, the priest says the following words of absolution: "May almighty God have mercy on us, forgive us our sins, and bring us to everlasting life." Notice that these words are different from the words of absolution we hear in the sacrament of reconciliation (confession). There, after we have confessed our sins and prayed an act of contrition, the priest says: "... and I absolve you from your sins, in the name of the Father and of the Son and of the Holy Spirit." In the Mass, then, the priest is *asking* God to forgive our sins, but in confession he is acting *in persona Christi* ("in the person of Christ"), with the authority given him by his ordination and his bishop to actually forgive our sins. Why is this important? Because it highlights our need for confession when we have committed serious (i.e., mortal) sins. Venial sins can be forgiven during Mass itself, in the Penitential Rite, and in our reception of the Holy Eucharist.

GRACE

In the glossary of the *Catechism of the Catholic Church* (page 881), grace is defined as:

> The free and undeserved gift that God gives us to respond to our vocation to become his adopted children. As sanctifying grace, God shares his divine life and friendship with us in a habitual gift, a stable and supernatural disposition that enables the soul to live with God, to act by his love. As actual grace, God gives us the help to conform our lives to his will. Sacramental grace and special graces (charisms, the grace of one's state of life) are gifts of the Holy Spirit to help us live out our Christian vocation.

Now, this is the *Catechism's glossary* definition—the one that simplifies the longer, trickier definitions. Does that tell you how theologically deep this little word "grace" is? (The *Catechism's* full presentation on grace is found in CCC 1996–2005.)

Simply put, grace is a share in the very life of God, which he gives us first through baptism and then through the other sacraments. Grace, then, is God's life in us. This is why the Mass and the Eucharist are so vital to our spiritual lives. They nourish and build up the life of grace within us, drawing us ever closer to the Holy Spirit.

Be aware that the Catholic understanding of grace differs—significantly in some respects—from the Protestant view. A non-Catholic Christian would not usually speak of grace as "God's life" living within them but rather as an external covering of sins through the blood of Christ. This unfortunate misunderstanding is important to note, because the Catholic understanding of grace impacts every part of our lives.

FIND IT

Jesus, the Bread of Life, was born in the town of Bethlehem. What does the name "Bethlehem" mean? (There is a hint in the question.)

We set the
Table.
God
is the one who
comes and does the
Work.

-MARK HART-

The Mystery Revealed

"Now as they were eating, Jesus took bread, and blessed, and broke it, and gave it to the disciples and said, 'Take, eat; this is my body.' And he took a cup, and when he had given thanks he gave it to them, saying, "Drink of it, all of you; for this is my blood of the covenant, which is poured out for many for the forgiveness of sins."

– Matthew 26:26-28

Lord Jesus, we hear these words during the consecration at every Mass. Help us to look beyond what we have seen and heard before. Through the intercession of Mary, your Mother, help us to think bigger. Help us to realize how much God loves us and to receive his love through the Eucharist.

We ask this through Christ our Lord.

Amen.

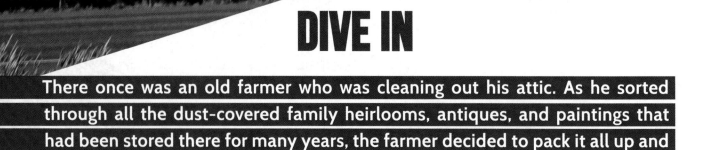

DIVE IN

There once was an old farmer who was cleaning out his attic. As he sorted through all the dust-covered family heirlooms, antiques, and paintings that had been stored there for many years, the farmer decided to pack it all up and sell (or trash) it.

He filled up his pickup truck and drove to town, hoping to make a few dollars. People came and looked over the stuff, but showed little interest in most of it. Finally, someone noticed an irregularity on one of the paintings. A corner of its canvas had been scratched away, revealing not a hole, but another canvas underneath.

Imagine everyone's surprise when a simple, dusty painting of a bowl of fruit was peeled back to reveal a stunning and priceless work of art from a famous Renaissance artist. The farmer, in shock, screamed with joy. Ultimately, he sold this masterpiece and returned to his farm a wealthy man.

"Jesus' presence is veiled."

As the saying goes, "One man's junk is another man's treasure." Not everyone believes that the Eucharist is truly Jesus' Body and Blood. Recent studies have shown that even many Catholics who attend Mass regularly do not believe—or at least "aren't sure"—that Christ is really and "substantially" present in the Eucharist. What about you? What do you believe the Eucharist is? A wafer of bread and a sip of wine? Or the true Body, Blood, Soul, and Divinity of Jesus Christ?

Consider the Communion host (or wafer) you receive at Mass. It does not look or taste like "normal" bread. But if you put it under a microscope and examine it, you would discover that, *from all appearances*, it is bread (though of a different kind than you might be used to).

Our Faith teaches us, though, that after the bread and wine are consecrated by the priest at Mass, what still looks and tastes like bread and wine has been transformed into Christ's Body and Blood. Jesus' presence is veiled; he is truly present "beneath the surface," hidden from our earthly eyes. Bread and wine now conceal history's greatest and perfect masterpiece, the Bread of Life, the Son of God.

Remember that most of Jesus' contemporaries did not accept him as the Messiah. It is possible for God to be in our midst, right in front of our eyes, and for us not to recognize him. So, look again now. Take a closer look—with faith—at the bread and wine and behold the Body and Blood of Christ.

DISCUSSION QUESTIONS

Segment 1: Lean In

What does Mark mean when he says Mass is "a collision of heaven and earth"?

_____

_____

_____

_____

Though we play a part in the Mass, it is more about what God is doing for us. Have you ever thought about the Mass as something God is doing rather than something we are doing?

_____

_____

_____

_____

Segment 2: The Greatest Gift

This program is called *Altaration*. What does Fr. Mike say that gives some idea of why this title was chosen?

_____

_____

_____

_____

Do you see Mass as an amazing, mysterious event or as just another Sunday "worship service," similar to those your non-Catholic friends may attend?

_____

_____

_____

_____

Do you take a few moments after receiving Communion to thank Jesus for what he has just given you—his very Body and Blood? Will you do that from now on?

_____

_____

_____

Segment 3: What If?

Were you surprised to learn that Mark had some of the same struggles many of you have? Have you ever had similar struggles?

_____

_____

_____

_____

During his confirmation retreat, Mark asked the question that changed his life: "What if?" Why do you think asking this question had such a profound impact on him?

_____

_____

_____

_____

If you really receive the Body and Blood of Christ in the Eucharist, what does that mean for how you should live your life?

_____

_____

_____

_____

FIND IT
What are the only Greek words used in the Mass? What do they mean?

ENTERING THE MYSTERY

At every Mass, we see our humanity and God's divinity meet as Jesus' sacrifice on the Cross and Last Supper are both made present on the altar in the Eucharist.

Have you ever considered this deep and mysterious reality?

Note that Jesus is not being *re-sacrificed* on the altar during Mass. His sacrifice on the Cross on Good Friday was a unique, unrepeatable, historical event. Its consequences, though—the liberation of every person who ever lived or will live from sin and death—are timeless and transcendent. In God's great love, Christ's sacrifice on Calvary is *re-presented* at every celebration of the Mass. When we go to Mass, we are not only witnessing what happened on Good Friday, we are transported to the Upper Room on Holy Thursday, when Jesus took bread and wine and offered them as his Body and Blood to his apostles, the first priests.

Now do you see why Mass is called a "mystery"?

There are visible and invisible realities transpiring at every Mass, just as there are in other areas of human experience.

Consider wind or love. In themselves, they are "invisible" realities, but you can see their effects. Though wind itself is invisible, we see flags and trees blowing and feel it on our faces, so we know it is present. Its effects are undeniable. Similarly, you cannot "see" love in itself, but you can see it being expressed in the care a mother gives to her child and in the affection a married couple shows toward one other.

God is like this. Strictly speaking, God is invisible to us on earth. But we can see his presence in the beauty of his creation—in majestic mountains, in the vastness of the oceans, in the seemingly limitless expanse of space, in the stars, in the profoundly complex mystery that is man. In a sense, nature is an evangelist pointing us to God like a compass points us north.

In the Incarnation, when God took on human flesh, the invisible God now had a visible face. When the apostles asked Jesus to show them the Father, he reminded them that, "He who has seen me has seen the Father" (John 14:9). Following Christ's ascension into heaven, we were given the Holy Spirit at Pentecost so that our "invisible God" could continue to make his presence known in visible ways through his Church.

Every Sunday and holy day, we proclaim the Nicene Creed, which begins: "I believe in one God, the Father almighty, maker of heaven and earth, of all things visible and invisible ..." Proclaiming him as the maker of things "visible and invisible" reminds us that God, as Creator, is constantly working and moving throughout creation. God is at work, and his work is for our salvation. The Mass is filled with actions, gestures, and movements where we see the visible and invisible "meet."

CHALLENGE

of the week

☐ Fast for an hour before Mass (the Church actually requires us to fast for an hour before receiving Communion). Dress up a little. Arrive at least fifteen minutes before Mass begins, and spend some time praying. Give thanks after receiving Communion. Pay attention to any difference these things make in your overall experience of the Mass.

Share your experience here:

_____

_____

_____

_____

_____

_____

_____

_____

_____

_____

_____

_____

_____

WRAP-UP

At every Mass we, in all our humanity, come to meet Jesus in the most real way possible. The hour that we set aside on Sunday, where we meet our Lord in the Eucharist, is actually the beginning of our week. It is the place where we bring God all the junk in our hearts, all our hopes and desires, and place them as an offering on the altar, and in return receive the food that brings us to everlasting life.

It is easy to become "mindless" in today's media-saturated world. Our brains are constantly stimulated by images and sounds, and it takes effort to escape the distractions. After a hard afternoon of practice or an intense night of studying, it is nice to fall on the couch, go mentally blank, and plug into the multimedia world. But, this makes it harder to develop a habit of prayer and can make it a challenge to "get quiet" during the ultimate prayer of the Mass.

Mass is the best opportunity you have during the week to quiet your soul, leave stress behind, and enter into a period of peaceful contemplation and reverence. Mass is certainly not a time to be "mindless." In fact, exactly the opposite is true: Mass should be the most "mindful" hour of your week, a time to contemplate *everything* that is going on in your life (engaging your mind, body, and soul) and listen to what God is saying.

The Mass is such a profound and amazing gift, that we should not just spend our time in the pew zoning out. We need to be focused on what is happening, listening to God's Word, and preparing ourselves to receive Jesus' Body and Blood in the Eucharist. And, after we receive Communion, we need to thank God for the infinite blessing he has just given us—his very self, a share in his very life.

You may be thinking, "Right, that all sounds nice, but I just can't wrap my head around any of it." That is OK. Just have the courage to ask the simple question, "What if?" ... and be prepared to see what God has in store for your life.

Closing Prayer

Jesus said, "I came that they may have life, and have it abundantly."
– John 10:10

Lord Jesus, you healed the blind and breathed light into the darkness. Thank you for helping us to see what you do for us during every Mass. May we never take for granted how much you love us or how incredible it is to receive you Body, Blood, Soul, and Divinity. Create in us a greater hunger for you, and make us open to the ways in which you want to bless our lives. Amen.

Any Questions?

Can I invite my non-Catholic friends to Mass?

Absolutely! Everyone is welcome to attend Mass. Of course, when a non-Catholic friend or family member comes with us to Mass, we hope that they have a great experience. We pray for good music, stellar preaching, and friendly faces. But we do need to prepare our non-Catholic guests ahead of time regarding Communion. We must gently and respectfully tell them that they should not get in line to receive the Eucharist.

But why are non-Catholics not invited to receive the Eucharist in the Catholic Church? Why are they excluded, even though Catholics may be invited to receive Communion in their churches? Unless you know and explain the reasons for this, your non-Catholic guests could incorrectly view this as a lack of hospitality or charity on the part of the Church. Nothing could be further from the truth.

In saying that non-Catholics may not receive the Eucharist, the Church is actually showing respect for their faith and beliefs and protecting them from receiving the Eucharist unworthily. When we as Catholics come forward to receive the Lord in Communion, the priest (or an extraordinary minister of the Eucharist) elevates the host and says, "The Body of Christ," to which we respond, "Amen."

This is our acknowledgment of our belief in Christ's real presence in the Eucharist, (i.e., that the bread we are about to receive is actually no longer bread but the very Body of Christ). By reserving reception of the Eucharist to those who have been formed in the Catholic Faith and share the Church's belief in the real presence, we are protecting the dignity of this great sacrament while at the same helping non-Catholics to remain faithful to their beliefs.

To allow those who do not share our Catholic Faith to receive Jesus in the Eucharist without fully understanding, believing, or proclaiming the same is actually a huge disservice to them. If they do not believe what the Church believes, then they should not be put in the awkward position of proclaiming, "Amen," to something they don't believe in.

If they do believe that Christ is truly present in the Eucharist *in the same sense that the Catholic Church does* (the phrase in italics is important, since many non-Catholic Christians believe that Jesus is "spiritually" or "symbolically" present), encourage them in their belief and gently ask if they have any questions about the Catholic Faith. Then, let the Holy Spirit guide them.

Ultimately, the best thing to do is to have this conversation with your non-Catholic family member or friend before Mass begins. Don't hesitate to invite anyone and everyone to Mass with you, and reassure them that they are always welcome. In doing so, you share the beauty and glory of the Lord's true presence in the Eucharist in such a way that they may see how significant it is in your life. This is the kind of witness St. Peter encourages us to make: "Always be prepared to make a defense to any one who calls you to account for the hope that is in you, yet do it with gentleness and reverence" (1 Peter 3:15).

Why do I have to give money to the Church?

We give money to the Church during Mass at the offertory as part of our sacrifice to God. In the early Church, the collection at Mass was taken up for the needs of the poor of the community. Today, the regular weekly Mass collection typically supports the day-to-day operations of the parish.

The money we give to our parish actually goes to a variety of things, including electricity and other utilities and the modest salaries of the parish staff and school, but mostly it goes toward serving those who give it. It supports all the various parish groups and activities, some of which you may participate in. (It is important to know that the cash or checks you put in the collection basket every week don't go to the priests. It is not like Father can use it to buy a sixty-inch HD TV for the rectory or a Porsche. Priests live very simply and are actually paid very little—and they also give money to the parish and to the poor.)

You may hear people criticize the Catholic Church for being "rich and extravagant" because of its beautiful churches and priceless works of art. They claim that such "wealth" is in contrast to the poverty of Jesus. Such a view, however, is ignorant and shortsighted. It is true that the Church owns precious art and stunning cathedrals, but in a very real sense, they belong not to the Church but to the entire world as a means of drawing people closer to the richness of God's truth. Just as the woman in the Gospel used expensive perfume to wash Jesus' feet, beautiful chalices, gorgeous stained glass, and stunning paintings and statues are intended to turn our hearts to sacred things.

In addition, no other organization on earth even comes close to the Catholic Church's level of charitable giving. Whether through its hospitals and schools, its work in developing countries, its food, housing, and clothing aid, or its work with the imprisoned, no one "out-gives" the Catholic Church.

Regarding our financial support of the Church, there is no specific amount you must give. That said, many parishes today operate on a "stewardship" model, where parishioners are encouraged to give of their time, talent, and treasure. In terms of the "treasure" part, some parishes encourage their parishioners to give ten percent of their income to the Church and other charities. (This is also referred to as "tithing,"

from the Old English term "tithe," meaning "tenth.") The amount of ten percent comes from the book of Genesis, where Abram (later Abraham) meets Melchizedek:

> Melchizedek king of Salem brought out bread and wine; he was priest of God Most High. And he blessed him and said, "Blessed be Abram by God Most High, maker of heaven and earth; and blessed be God Most High, who has delivered your enemies into your hand!" and Abram gave him a tenth of everything" (Genesis 14:18-20).

Notice that Abram gives a tenth of *everything*. This should be a model for us. It is a way of reminding us that we must never put creation above the Creator nor forget where all our gifts ultimately come from (see James 1:17). Recall how much God has blessed you, and prayerfully give back to him—and his Church—what you can.

WHAT'S THAT WORD?

ELEVATION

At various points in the Mass, you will see several items raised up, or elevated. Whether it is the elevation of the crucifix in the entrance procession, the elevation of the Book of Gospels by the priest (or deacon) as he processes to the *ambo* to read the Gospel, or the elevation of the sacred host during the consecration, things are regularly being "lifted up."

The elevation of the host and chalice during the Eucharistic Prayer is the most important of the actions. It is intended to draw our eyes to the sanctuary and also serve as a reminder of the various "elevations" in the Bible that symbolize and point to the Eucharist: Moses lifting up the healing serpent in the desert (see Numbers 21:4-9) and Christ being raised up and nailed upon the Cross to redeem us from our sins. Alluding to his future death on the Cross, Jesus himself recounts the story of Moses and the serpent during his late-night discussion with Nicodemus (see John 3:14–16).

In the thirteenth century, St. Eudes de Sully, a French bishop, began elevating the gifts in a pronounced way during the Liturgy. If you look closely, you will actually notice five elevations during Mass, both minor (subtle) and major (noticeable), to signify something important happening. These elevations make present the past and propel us toward the future throughout the timelessness of the Liturgy.

EPICLESIS

During Mass, have you ever noticed when the priest extends his hands over the gifts (i.e., the bread and wine) upon the altar and brings them down in a sweeping motion? This liturgical moment is called the *epiclesis* (which is Greek for "calling down upon"), and it is a powerful symbol of the priest "calling down" the Holy Spirit upon the gifts so that they might be transformed into Christ's Body and Blood.

Like the Old Testament prophet Elijah almost three thousand years ago, the priest stands at an altar, one built on twelve (apostolic) stones. God rained down power, wind, and fire from heaven to consume Elijah's sacrifice, and during the *epiclesis*, the Holy Spirit descends in power to consume and transform our sacrifices of bread, wine, monetary offerings, and prayer that have been brought to the altar.

LAVABO

Have you ever noticed when the priest "pauses" to wash his hands at the beginning of the Liturgy of the Eucharist? An altar server is usually there to pour water over the priest's hands and offer him a towel. The basin or bowl used to wash the priest's hands is called the *lavabo* (Latin for "I will wash"). During this moment of ceremonial washing, the priest quotes from the prayer of King David in Psalm 51:2: "Lord, wash away my iniquity, and cleanse me from my sin." In this liturgical action, the priest is imploring God's mercy for his own sinfulness, asking that he be purified to celebrate the Eucharist.

You are sent.

CHRIS STEFANICK

What is Our Response?

"And Jesus came and said to them, 'All authority in heaven and on earth has been given to me. Go therefore and make disciples of all nations, baptizing them in the name of the Father and of the Son and of the Holy Spirit, teaching them to observe all that I have commanded you; and lo, I am with you always, to the close of the age.'"

– Matthew 28:18-20

Lord, you promised to be with us always. Thank you for being a Father who keeps his promises. Help us to trust in your words. Give us a spirit of confidence and humble boldness not only to believe we are your children but to act like it. May we never doubt your presence within our lives or in the Eucharist. May our lives be a living witness to the mysterious reality taking place upon the altar at every Mass.

We ask this through Christ our Lord.

Amen.

DIVE IN

The television was on, but I wasn't really watching it. My little brother was playing with his ninja turtles in the corner, and my parents kept asking me if I was feeling OK. I sat on the couch with my headphones on, without listening to any music, trying to make sense of my "crumbling" seventeen-year-old life.

It was a Saturday night. I had cash in my pocket and gas in my truck, but the phone was not ringing. The silence was a deafening reminder of how sad my social life had become practically overnight. I no longer had any friends. This was something new for me. In my previous three years of high school, I never sat home on a Saturday night. I expected that my senior year would be epic, socially speaking. Instead, it had become increasingly lonely, and there was only one person to blame—Jesus.

At one point, I think I actually said, "Jesus, you ruined my senior year."

During the prior six months, I had several powerful encounters with Jesus on two different retreats. I knew that I had to make some major changes in my life if I really wanted to become who God was calling me to be. So I did. I broke up with my girlfriend, and I quit drinking. I cleaned up my language and changed my attitude.

I began sharing Christ with my friends ... a move that quickly revealed how few true friends I really had. I got more involved in my church, and I changed the music I listened to and the movies I watched. I learned to pray. I began going to Eucharistic Adoration. The Holy Spirit turned my world upside down, and many people who had been within it decided they wanted nothing to do with me or my newfound "best friend," Jesus.

So there I was, at home on a Saturday night, trying to be a "good person." No one had told me what would happen if I got serious about following God. No one had told me that there would be really lonely nights sometimes. No one told me that the devil would come after me harder than ever, trying to distract me from my relationship with Christ.

Here is the part of the story where you might be expecting a happy ending. Maybe the phone rang and my youth group friends invited me out, or perhaps my parents and I had our first profound discussion about God, life, death, and eternity. Something like this happened, right?

Nope. No happy ending ... not for a while, anyway. I was lonely, but God was allowing it for a reason (though I didn't know it at the time). It turned out that I needed some time alone to grow in character and in virtue. So God separated me from some bad influences and tempting relationships in order to strengthen me. He invited me out of a sinful environment to help get sinful desires out of my heart.

After awhile I made some new friends ... *true* friends ... you know, the kind who stand with you, walk with you, and challenge you to become a better person. I realized that God hadn't called me to be a "good person" or a "better version" of me but a *new* person (see Galatians 2:20), one who could fulfill the design he had for me (see Ephesians 2:10). God was calling me to a deeper relationship and true intimacy, but he first had to reveal all the false relationships in my life.

In time, I realized how important it was for me to feel this period of loneliness during my senior year. It taught me how to lean on Christ and not just on my friends. I had been betrayed, gossiped about, mocked, and abandoned ... just like Jesus (though not nearly to the same degree). No one in my life, except Christ, could really understand me or the person he was recreating me to be.

What about you?

Have you heard God calling you to make some changes? Maybe you spent a week at camp, attended a youth conference, or went on a mission trip and encountered God in a new way. What now? Know that the devil will try everything in his power to distract you from God and from making a true, lasting change in your life. He will seek to demoralize you, to convince you it was all "just a phase." He will whisper lie after lie in your ear. I know, because I went through all of this. I began to believe his lies—but then I remembered that I wasn't really alone. Jesus was right with me through it all.

Remember that even if everyone is against you, Jesus is always with you. You are never alone. Jesus is with you every second of every day, and you can turn to him in prayer whenever you need to. In addition, he speaks to you in the Scriptures. He is present to you in the Church. He meets you at every Mass. As he promised the apostles, "I am with you always, to the close of the age" (Matthew 28:20).

I can't imagine my life without Christ. I wouldn't even want to. In Jesus, I have experienced more freedom and joy than I can even begin to express. You can experience this same joy and freedom as well.

DISCUSSION QUESTIONS

Segment 1: I Do

Have you ever thought about yourself as a "bride of Christ"? Probably not. But does it make sense that if Jesus is the divine Groom and the Church is his bride, then we, as members of the Church, are united to him?

Yes it does make sense.

When you walk down the aisle to receive the Eucharist, you are on your way to become one with God. How will this new understanding impact the way you approach the altar?

Take it more seriously.

Segment 2: Sent Forth

Chris points out that the word "Mass" comes from the Latin phrase *Ite, missa est.* What does this phrase literally mean? What does it mean to you? Have you ever thought about how the week actually begins with Sunday Mass, where we are sent out into the world to bring Christ's love?

It means to be sent to go to mass.

How do you think St. John Paul II was able to forgive the man who shot him? Have you ever given or received such profound forgiveness?

He was able to forgive the man by asking God for help

Blessed Frassati said, "God comes to visit me every day in the Eucharist. I return the favor by visiting the poor." Do you see the face of God in those in need?

Yes.

_____

_____

Where did Blessed Teresa of Calcutta (Mother Teresa) get the strength to work under such difficult conditions? Do you turn to God during challenging times?

Got her Strength from God

_____

_____

Have you ever thought about your home or your school as a "mission field," where you are called to bring the love of God to those that need it? How could you do this?

_NO_

_____

_____

_____

Segment 3: Will You Let Him?

What does Mark mean when he says that we are all "called to be saints"? Have you ever thought of yourself as a "saint in the making"? Why, or why not?

_____

_____

_____

_____

In Mark's words, "The power to change the world flows off of the altar." What does this mean? How might it change the way you approach Mass?

_____

_____

_____

_____

Do you see the Church as a solid foundation that is immovable? Are Christ and the Church your foundation? If not, what is?

_____

_____

_____

_____

ENTERING THE MYSTERY

The year was 1244, and Holy Roman Emperor Frederick II was at war with the pope—and, by extension, the Church.

Frederick sent his armies throughout Italy and planned to attack several Catholic communities, including the small town of Assisi. St. Clare was quite ill and confined to her convent bed at the time. But when news of the invading army reached her, Clare asked the priest to bring the Eucharist to her bedside.

St. Clare prayed. Suddenly filled with strength, she rose from her bed "armed" only with the Lord. A small, sickly nun was about to confront an army of thousands with a consecrated host.

As the soldiers began to surround the convent and approach its towering walls, St. Clare stood on the roof and elevated the Blessed Sacrament as she prayed, "I beseech thee, Good Lord, protect these whom now I am not able to protect!"

At that moment, witnesses say the invaders stopped dead in their tracks, their faces became almost ghostly white, and they fell back from the walls, as if they had been struck by lightning. Such is the power of the Eucharist.

Some other examples of the Eucharist's power: St. Joseph of Cupertino (1603–1663) would often levitate during Mass, literally flying through the air because he was so overcome with love for the now-present Eucharistic Lord. When he celebrated Mass, St. Philip Neri (1515–1595) would sometimes have sparks shoot out of his eyes and off of his hands during the consecration. St. Teresa of Avila (1515–1582) would become so physically overwhelmed during Communion that she often entered into an ecstatic state and was unable to move after receiving the Lord; she needed help to walk (or be carried) out of the chapel, hours after Mass had ended. Blessed Alexandria Maria da Costa (1904–1955) was bedridden and unable to eat any food other than the Eucharist, which she received every day. The Lord was *literally* her daily bread.

There is real power in the Eucharist.

These are just a handful of the innumerable events that have occurred over the two-thousand-year history of the Church. These stories are not legends but historical events, corroborated by witnesses and typically recorded in great detail. These events, which span the globe and transcend cultures, languages, time periods, and social classes, have one thing in common—the Eucharist.

Consider that the same Eucharist that stopped armies, caused saints to levitate, and sustained the seriously ill is made present to you at every Mass. The same God who worked these miracles throughout history works a miracle for you through the same priesthood and the same words of consecration in every Catholic church on the planet, in every language, every day.

The saints enjoyed such great intimacy with God because they desired to know him and be known by him with their whole hearts. They experienced indescribable, external miracles because they allowed the Lord to work equally powerful but less obvious miracles within them, in their hearts. It was this spiritual intimacy that led to physical miracles, and it is that same intimacy that the Lord offers you every Sunday at Mass.

As a member of the Catholic Church, you are invited to a "wedding feast" (see Matthew 22:1-14) at every Mass. Not as a distant relative but as the guest of honor! When St. Paul calls the Church "the bride" of Christ (see Ephesians 5:23-25), he gives us incredible insight not only into our worth but also into God's unfathomable love. For just as a man and woman become one with each other during the sacrament of holy matrimony, the Church becomes one with Christ through the Blessed Sacrament at every Mass. In essence, every Mass is a wedding celebration and, as such, it offers you what God offered all of these (and many more) saints—true intimacy.

You will never know what you are capable of or how strong the Lord can be within you until you accept his invitation to become one with him at Mass. Then, and only then, will you come to know your true worth, your true strength, and your true peace.

There is real power in the Eucharist.

CHALLENGE

of the **week**

☐ Invite a friend or family member to attend Mass with you. If the person accepts, be sure to be a good example (e.g., really enter into prayer, pay attention, dress well, and sing). If the person declines your invitation, don't take it personally, but just pray for him or her during Mass. Invite them again in the future. Remember to mention the Church's teaching on reception of the Eucharist (as was discussed in the "Any Questions" section of Session Three on page 38).

Share your experience here:

_____

_____

_____

_____

_____

_____

_____

_____

_____

_____

_____

_____

_____

WRAP-UP

Here comes the bride, all dressed in white ... OK, I know thinking of yourself as a "bride" at Mass can seem very weird at first, especially for you guys. This wedding imagery might seem awkward, but it is God's idea.

Throughout Scripture, the union between a husband and wife is the most frequently used analogy for the kind of relationship God desires with us. In marriage, a couple is called to mutual self-sacrifice and faithful, fruitful love. Consider, then, how a holy marriage, in which each spouse offers his or her body to the other as a gift, can be seen reflected in the Mass, where God offers us his very Body and asks us to offer him our whole selves—our bodies, minds, and talents—as a gift. These are deep and mystical realities, and if you are open to them, you will see more clearly how much God loves you and how much Jesus has done for you ... offering up his Body for you so that you may live. Isn't that what any good husband would do for his bride?

The gifts God gives us are immeasurable. Now that we know the depths of what is before us on the altar, it is clear we cannot just keep this amazing truth to ourselves. We are called to go out into the world spreading peace and the message of God's saving grace to everyone we meet. It has been said that Christ has no other hands but yours, no other lips but yours, no other feet but yours. He wants to work through you to bring hope to a hurting world. The question is, will you let him?

Closing Prayer

"Behold, I send you out as sheep in the midst of wolves; so be wise as serpents and innocent as doves."

- Matthew 10:16

Lord Jesus, thank your for this journey that we have been on to discover the meaning and purpose behind the mystery of the Mass. We are grateful to have gained new perspective on what it all really means. Help us to make what we have learned a part of our lives, so that we can grow in our relationship with you and be a witness of your love to all those we come in contact with. Please lead us, guide us, and protect us always. Amen.

Any Questions?

How long am I supposed to fast before Mass? Why must I do this?

Have you ever looked at a clock on Sunday morning with your stomach growling and then done the math in your head to see if you could eat something quickly before running out to Mass? If you are like most Catholics, you have probably done this a few times in your life.

We are required to fast "for *at least one hour* before holy communion from any food and drink, except for only water and medicine" (Code of Canon Law 919, emphasis added). Many Catholics fast for an hour before Mass begins or even the entire morning until after Mass has ended. Be aware that "back in the day" (before 1964), Catholics had to fast from midnight until they received the Eucharist the following morning. So we are getting off lightly today!)

But why do we do this? We do this to unite our sacrifice (i.e., fasting for an hour) in a very small way with Christ's sacrifice on the Cross, which we celebrate at Mass. Fasting helps train our bodies to follow the lead of our souls, to allow our spirit to lead our flesh and not vice versa. Fasting before Mass helps ensure that we come to church hungry, both physically and spiritually, so that Christ—and nothing else—can satisfy our hunger.

Why should I stay until the end of Mass? I see many people leave after Communion.

Communion is not the end of Mass. In fact, the time of meditation and prayer following Communion should be one of the most important moments for us within the Mass—and even our entire week. The Eucharistic meditation provides us with unrivaled intimacy and spiritual communion (as you already heard about in Session Three).

In addition, the final blessing after Communion confers grace upon us that we will need during the week to live out the challenges the Scripture readings and homily have just given us. The recessional song at the end of Mass is a wonderful opportunity to raise our voices and celebrate God's greatness and love one last time. Out of respect, we should wait to leave until the priest and ministers have left the sanctuary and processed out. There is also a rich symbolism here of "following Christ out into the world."

In short, if we really understood what is transpiring at Mass, we would not be in such a hurry to leave. We would embrace every minute and every chance we have to stay in God's Eucharistic presence, surrounded by our fellow Christians.

Those who regularly leave Mass early probably do not really understand and appreciate the

great gift they have just been a part of. Your prayerful example of remaining until after the priest and ministers have left the sanctuary will be an example to others, inspiring them to take a second look at their own practice.

Is it really a sin to miss Mass?

A Catholic friend of mine once offered his opinion on why the Church requires us to attend Mass every Sunday: "Well, of course the pope is going to say that missing Mass is a sin. He wants to be sure people keep going and putting money in the basket." This was his explanation as to why the Church teaches that missing Mass intentionally and without good reason (e.g., sickness, family crisis, work) is a serious sin.

"For where your treasure is, there will your heart be also." (Matthew 6:21-23)

Leaving my friend's rather cynical (and obviously false) view aside, why does the Church teach that it is a serious sin to miss Mass? The Mass is our source of eternal life; it is the fountain of grace for our dehydrated and self-absorbed souls. Like a grape that withers and dies when cut off from the lifeblood of the vine, so we slowly wither—dying a slow death from sin—when we are not in regular communion with the grace and life of God's vine. So emphatic was Christ of our need for the Father that he used this analogy of the vine and the branches (see John 15:1-6).

Sin is death, as St. Paul tells us (see Romans 6:23). This is not meant figuratively or metaphorically; sinning seriously against God literally kills his grace within us. The saints all preferred physical death (and even martyrdom, in many case) to sin. Jesus reminds us not to fear physical death but rather spiritual death through sin (see Matthew 10:28).

Remember than an objectively mortal sin is one that concerns a "grave" (or serious) matter, typically a moral issue. The Church, which acts with the authority given it by Jesus himself, has appropriately made attending Mass on Sundays and holy days of obligation a "grave" matter, basing this on the third commandment to "keep holy" the Sabbath day (see Exodus 20:8; CCC 2168–2188). One must *know* of this obligation and *freely decide* to skip Mass *without a valid reason* (e.g., illness, taking care of a sick family member, or a necessary work obligation) for one to be guilty of a serious sin.

Missing Mass doesn't just "happen." Choosing to sleep in, go to a game, meet friends for breakfast, or just "hang out" on a Sunday morning may sound great—but not if any of these activities take the place of Mass. In effect, what we are saying when we make time for other things but not for Mass is that *[fill in the activity]* is actually our "god" on Sunday rather than Jesus. We need to remember Jesus' words, "For where your treasure is, there will your heart be also" (Matthew 6:21).

Fortunately, most parishes offer several Masses on Sundays (including a Saturday evening vigil) to accommodate parishioners' busy schedules. So, yes, skipping Mass is objectively a serious sin. But the real question is not whether we sin when we skip Mass but rather what we are missing when we do so—an encounter with the living God, with Jesus in the Eucharist.

FIND IT

If your parish does not have Eucharistic Adoration, find the nearest church or chapel in your area that does. Make a visit for at least thirty minutes. Simply talk to Jesus from your heart and listen to what he wants to say to you.

Write the name of the Church and the day and time you prayed there.

WHAT'S THAT WORD?

MONSTRANCE

From a Latin term meaning "to show forth," a monstrance is the sacred vessel in which the Eucharistic host is exhibited for Adoration. (In the video we just watched, Fr. Louis was carrying a monstrance as he processed past the teens.)

Monstrances are intentionally and carefully handcrafted to draw our eyes and lift our hearts as we adore the Eucharist. They can have different designs, but the most common form is of a sun or starburst, to symbolize the radiance of Christ's glory in the Eucharist. They are usually made of a precious metal (e.g., gold or silver), though some are wood. A monstrance is often placed on an elevated platform to raise it higher.

The monstrance can also serve as a powerful analogy to our own lives in Christ. When we seek the Eucharist, hunger for it, and go frequently to Mass and Eucharistic Adoration, we fulfill our purpose—we *literally* have Christ at the center of our lives. When we lose communion with the Eucharist, we become like an empty monstrance—handcrafted by God, shiny and beautiful, but empty. Without Christ, we are unable to fulfill the purpose for which he has created us.

The more we understand that God wants to dwell within us, the more intentional we can be about making ourselves (our "monstrance") a worthy dwelling place for him. This often requires that we take a prayerful look at our lives and discover where we need to be reconciled with God.

CONSUBSTANTIAL

This somewhat technical-sounding, philosophical term is used in the Nicene Creed we pray at Mass to refer to Jesus, the Son of God, being "of the same substance" as God the Father: "I believe in one Lord Jesus Christ, the Only Begotten Son of God, born of the Father before all ages. God from God, Light from Light, true God from true God, begotten, not made, *consubstantial* with the Father; through him all things were made."

In the year 325, the early Church Fathers met at Nicaea, a city in what is modern-day Turkey, in the Church's first ecumenical council. Their task was to clarify the relationship between God the Father and Jesus Christ, God the Son. There were some people at the time teaching that Jesus was "of *similar* substance" as the Father (i.e., that he was special but not really God). The bishops, under the guidance of the Holy Spirit, declared that Jesus is rather "of *the same* substance" as the Father, (i.e., that he is God). This doctrine of the Church is expressed in the word "consubstantial." As

Jesus told his apostles, "The Father and I are one" (John 10:30, NAB).

The Church teaches that Christ is consubstantial (that is, "of the same substance") with the Father because he is fully God. He is not "partially God" or "like God." He shares the same divine nature as God the Father and the Holy Spirit. Thus, Jesus Christ is of the same "substance" as the Father and the Holy Spirit.

The Church has defined such terms to help us understand something of the mystery of the Holy Trinity. Since God is infinite, though, and we are his finite creation, we will never understand God's essence. We can simply try to understand as best we can what he has revealed to us about himself. Check out CCC 242, 262, 467, and 663 to go a little deeper.

TRANSUBSTANTIATION

We Catholics love big words: *"epiclesis,"* "doxology," "catechesis," "Magisterium." Perhaps the biggest—and most misunderstood—of all is "transubstantiation."

Transubstantiation is the theological term used to describe what happens at every Mass during the consecration of the bread and wine. The gifts of bread and wine are *substantially* changed into the true Body and Blood of Jesus Christ when the priest, by the power of the Holy Spirit, proclaims the words of consecration (see CCC 1373–1377). The very *substance* of the bread and wine is changed, though they continue to look, feel, taste, and smell like ordinary bread and wine. This leads some to falsely conclude that if Jesus is present in the Eucharist, he can only be spiritually—not physically—present in it.

So how do we, as Catholics, explain our belief in the real presence of Christ in the Eucharist? Well, we can start by pointing out that there are two "components" of every material object: its "substance" and its "accidents" (used here in a technical sense, not in the way we use it in everyday speech). The substance is the very *essence* of what a thing is (i.e., what it *really is* at its core). A thing's "accidents" are aspects of it that adhere to it but are not essential to it—for example, its size and how it looks, tastes, feels, and smells.

You and I are human beings—that is our "essence," or substance. You may be younger than I am, or shorter, or taller, or have a different hair color, or be a better athlete or musician; but these are just "accidental" characteristics of what we really are—human beings.

The miracle of the Eucharist, though, is that the accidents of the bread and wine remain (i.e., they look, smell, and taste the same), but through the power of the Holy Spirit, their substance has been miraculously changed into Christ's Body and Blood. The Eucharist is not a mystery to be solved, but a mystery to behold.

When you receive Holy Communion, you become a kind of "walking tabernacle," carrying God himself within you in the most intimate way possible. You become a temple of his very life and grace. The Eucharist truly has the power to change you like nothing else on earth.

To go even deeper, check out what the *Catechism* has to say about it: CCC 1373–1377, 1404, and 1413.

EVERYTHING WE DO MEANS SOMETHING

FR. MIKE SCHMITZ

The "Whys" Behind the "Whats"

"The cup of blessing which we bless, is it not a participation in the blood of Christ? The bread which we break, is it not a participation in the body of Christ? Because there is one bread, we who are many are one body for we all partake of the one bread."

– 1 Corinthians 10:16-17

Lord Jesus, in this program, we have been on a journey and have come to see that things are not always what they seem. We have discovered that there is so much more going on at Mass than we realized. Even if we still do not fully understand what we have learned, thank you for opening our eyes to this profound mystery of our Faith. Help us continue to "see" and come to believe that we are fully united with you and each other in the gift of the Mass.

We ask this through Christ our Lord.

Amen.

DIVE IN

We have been on a journey to discover the mystery of the Mass and our role in bringing the graces we have received in the Eucharist to a needy world.

This week, we are going to take a closer look at the actual parts of the Mass. Fr. Mike Schmitz will walk us through the deeper meaning behind the words and actions you have witnessed thousands of times. Let's dig in.

VIDEO NOTES

Everything we do means something. Each season is a color. Mass is about Jesus

Why we Geneflect

1.) Going to one knee is honoring God

We stand because we are part of the pilgrimage.

God is a trinity

your tracing your worth The Sign of the cross reminds you that you love him. Bring something to write with and on. The priest makes a sielent prayer Alleula means to praise to God. The first word for the creed is I believe.

The sign of peace

ENTERING THE MYSTERY

We consume many things in the course of an average day: food, water, air.

But our consumption is not limited to what we eat, drink, or breathe. We consume media and information, too. We even say that people are "consumed" with guilt or pain. When we buy something, we are called "consumers."

The word "consume" comes from the Latin term *consumere* (*con* means "together" and *sumere* means "taken up"). So when something is consumed, it is literally "taken up" by or into something else. When we grill a hamburger, the flames would consume the meat if it were not for the metal rack it sits on. Instead, after it is cooked, the burger will be consumed by a person. Either way, that hamburger will be consumed or "taken up" by something.

Some things that we consume lead us to heaven. Other things we consume point us toward hell. Think about it. It is really that simple.

We consume whatever we eat, drink, watch, or buy, and, all too often, we are consumed by these things. Good and evil, virtue and vice are in a tug of war for our souls, and the decisions we make in terms of what we consume play a huge role in what side wins the battle. It is not that things are inherently evil; rather, our sinful misuse of them is. We can make things our "gods," the true desires of our hearts, instead of God. As Jesus warns us:

> Do not lay up for yourselves treasures on earth, where moth and rust consume and where thieves break in and steal, but store up for yourselves treasures in heaven, where neither moth nor rust consumes and where thieves do not break in and steal. For where your treasure is, there will your heart be also" (Matthew 6:19-21).

Our culture today is in bad shape because our hearts seek to consume the wrong "treasure"—and because we are so consumed with self.

The Mass, though, is not "all about us." Even the most self-absorbed "consumer" is called to look beyond his or her own self and focus on God. Jesus wants us to bring our hopes, fears, and sins to Mass, to unite our needs and sufferings to his on the Cross. In the Mass, we seek to be consumed by the Father's love instead of the enemy's lies; we seek heaven rather than earth.

When we walk forward to receive Communion, we walk toward the altar of sacrifice, where the Holy Spirit, through the ministry of the priest, has transformed (or, more technically, "transubstantiated") bread and wine into Christ's very Body and Blood. In receiving the Eucharist, however, our "consumption" is more than what we see.

While we "consume" Christ in the Eucharist, Christ is also consuming us with his grace. If we are properly disposed to receive him, Jesus literally changes us from the inside out. Through Communion, we are given a "divine blood transfusion" and a "spiritual heart transplant." God raises us to new heights, "taking us up altogether" to give us a glimpse—a foretaste—of heaven.

Before you receive the Eucharist next, ask the Holy Spirit to consume your mind and heart with wisdom, so that you might really see "who is consuming whom" at Mass.

CHALLENGE

of the week

Now that you know all the parts and players of the Mass, get out of the pew and get involved. Consider all the possible ways you could assist at Mass—as a lector, usher, cantor, musician, or altar server, among other roles—and ask God for help to discern your gifts. Then find the right contact, usually listed in the bulletin, and inquire about getting involved. Remember, you are part of the Church, and the Church needs you!

Share your experience here:

_____

_____

_____

_____

_____

_____

_____

_____

_____

_____

_____

_____

_____

WRAP-UP

The more you "get into" your faith and, more specifically, the Mass, two things will inevitably happen.

First, you will want to learn more about it. Be sure to keep reading and studying about the Mass. You might want to check out books such as *Behold the Mystery: A Deeper Understanding of the Catholic Mass* by Mark Hart and *Do I Have to Go: 101 Questions About the Mass, the Eucharist, and Your Spiritual Life* by Chris Stefanick and Matthew Pinto.

Second, the Lord will increasingly use you to evangelize others—Catholics and non-Catholics alike—about the incredible gift of the Mass. For that reason, keep this workbook and come back to it after the study is over. Refer to the definitions, lists, and explanations. Take the time to commit different terms and concepts to memory, and watch as the Lord brings people into your life who are searching for the answers you now possess.

Closing Prayer

[Jesus said to his disciples,] "He who eats my flesh and drinks my blood has eternal life, and I will raise him up at the last day. For my flesh is food indeed, and my blood is drink indeed. He who eats my flesh and drinks my blood abides in me, and I in him. As the living Father sent me, and I live because of the Father, so he who eats me will live because of me. This is the bread which came down from heaven, not such as the fathers ate and died; he who eats this bread will live for ever." ... Many of his disciples, when they heard it, said, "This is a hard saying; who can listen to it?" ... After this many of his disciples drew back and no longer went about with him. Jesus said to the twelve, "Will you also go away?" Simon Peter answered him, "Lord, to whom shall we go? You have the words of eternal life."

– John 6:54-58, 60, 66-68

Lord, we have learned many things and grown much in our study of the Mass. Some were easy. Some were hard. Help us never to be afraid of anything that you want to teach us or do in and through us. Thank you for always being patient with us and loving us despite our faults and sins. Help us in our moments of doubt to believe that you are the Way, the Truth, and the Life, and that you are truly present in the Eucharist as real, eternal food. Thank you for giving us the Mass as a way to be in personal communion with you. Help us to fully enter in, never take it for granted, and be your disciples. Amen.

Any Questions?

Why does the priest preach the homily after the Gospel reading?

Simply put, the homily is intended to be a reflection on the Bible readings (or at least *one* of the readings, usually the Gospel) that have just been proclaimed. Though the essential meaning of the Bible is for every age and culture, it was written thousands of years ago to people whose everyday lives and customs were very different from our own. For example, how do we reach out to lepers when there do not seem to be any hanging out in front of our local coffee shop? In his homily, the priest or deacon seeks to help us understand the sometimes confusing context of the readings so that we can understand the Bible's wisdom and know its implications for us to live the gospel more faithfully.

St. Paul, in writing to the Thessalonians, discusses the importance of receiving and living out the Word: "We also thank God constantly for this, that when you received the word of God which you heard from us, you accepted it not as the word of men but as what it really is, the word of God, which is at work in you believers" (1 Thessalonians 2:13). The homily ought to help us live out God's Word more intentionally in deed and not merely in thought.

Do I have to go to confession before receiving Communion?

The short answer: If you are conscious of committing a serious sin, then you must go to confession before receiving Communion. Now, let's unpack the reasons the Church requires this.

> St. Paul offers the church in Corinth a pretty convincing reason: "Whoever, therefore, eats the bread or drinks the cup of the Lord in an unworthy manner will be guilty of profaning the Body and Blood of the Lord. Let a man examine himself, and so eat of the bread and drink of the cup. For any one who eats and drinks without discerning the body eats and drinks judgment upon himself" (1 Corinthians 11:27-29).

Imagine yourself on Christmas morning opening your presents. Your father gives you a special gift that cost him his life savings. He hands it to you with great care. You are overwhelmed by its beauty, not only of the gift itself but of the great sacrifice and love that are behind it. You are speechless that such a wonderful gift has been entrusted to you. Would you just unwrap it, toss it over your shoulder, and move on to the next present? Of course not. Why? Because doing so would make absolutely no sense.

Our actions follow our beliefs. If we believe something is a gift, we handle it with great care and give it the respect it deserves. By extension,

serious (i.e., mortal) sin, in effect, pushes God's sanctifying grace from our soul; it suffocates his life within us. If we have committed a mortal sin that has not been forgiven, we need to confess it so we are prepared to receive the perfect, stainless, and unfathomable gift of the Eucharist. The sacrament of reconciliation restores us to

God's sanctifying grace and prepares us to be a proper receptacle for the Body and Blood of the Lord. Confessing our sins transforms us, once again, into a monstrance—a "mobile tabernacle" ready and able to bring Christ's Eucharistic presence into the world.

FIND IT

Name all of the liturgical seasons in the Church calendar and the color associated with each. Can you explain the meaning of each season and color?

(Hint: Answers can be found in the "Resources for Diving in Deeper" section of this workbook.)

MY SIDE OF THE CONFESSIONAL

BY FR. MIKE SCHMITZ (COURTESY OF LIFETEEN INTERNATIONAL)

Once, when traveling, I was riding a shuttle bus with a number of older folks on the way to the airport. They noticed that I was a priest, and they started asking me some questions.

"Do you do all of the 'priest stuff'?"

"Yep."

"Even the confession thing?"

"Yeah. All the time."

One older lady gasped, "Well, I think that that would be the *worst*. It would be so depressing, hearing all about people's sins."

I told them that it is just the opposite. There is almost no greater place to be than with someone when they are coming back to God. I said, "It would depressing if I had to watch someone leave God; I get to be with them when they come back to him." In confession, people let God's love win. The confessional is the most joyful, humbling, and inspiring place in the world.

WHAT DO I SEE IN CONFESSION?

I think there are three things. First, I see the costly mercy of God in action. I get to regularly come face to face with the overwhelming, life-transforming power of God's love. I get to see God's love up close, and it reminds me of how good God is.

Not many folks get to see the way in which Jesus' sacrifice on the Cross is constantly breaking into people's lives and melting the hardest hearts. Jesus consoles those who are grieving their sins ... and strengthens those who find themselves wanting to give up on God or on life.

As a priest, I get to see this thing happen *every day*.

I SEE A SAINT IN THE MAKING.

The second thing I see is a person who is still trying—a saint in the making. I don't care if this is the person's third confession this week; if they are seeking the sacrament of reconciliation, it means that they are trying. That is all that I care about. This thought is worth considering: Going to confession is a sign that you haven't given up on Jesus.

This is one of the reasons why pride is so deadly. I have talked with people who tell me that they do not want to go to confession to their pastor because he really likes them and "thinks that they are a good kid."

I have two things to say to this:

He will not be disappointed! What your priest will see is a person who is trying. I dare you to find a saint who didn't need God's mercy. (Even Mary needed God's mercy. She received the mercy of God in a dramatic and powerful way at her conception.)

So what if the priest is disappointed? We try to be so impressive with so much of our lives. Confession is a place where we don't get to be impressive. Confession is a place where the desire to impress goes to die. Think about it: All other sins have the potential to cause us to race to the confessional, but pride is the one that causes us to hide from the God who could heal us.

DO I REMEMBER YOUR SINS? NO!

People often ask me if I remember people's sins from confession. As a priest, I rarely, if ever, remember sins from the confessional. That might seem impossible, but the truth is, sins are not all that impressive. They are not like memorable sunsets, meteor showers, super-intriguing movies ... they are more like garbage.

So if sins are like garbage, then a priest is like God's garbage man. If you ask a garbage man about the grossest thing he has ever had to haul to the dump, *maybe* he could remember it. The fact is, though, when you get used to taking out the trash, it ceases to be noteworthy, it ceases to stand out.

Honestly, once you realize that the sacrament of reconciliation is less about the sins confessed and more about Christ's death and resurrection being victorious in a person's life, then the sins lose all of their luster, and Jesus' victory takes center stage.

In confession, we meet the life-transforming, costly love of God ... freely given to us every time we ask for it. We meet Jesus, who reminds us, "You are worth dying for ... even in your sins, you are worth dying for."

Whenever someone comes to confession, I see a person who is deeply loved by God and who is telling God that they love him. That's it.

IN CONFESSION, I SEE MY OWN WEAKNESS.

The third thing a priest sees when he hears confessions is his own soul. I cannot tell you how humbled I am when someone approaches Jesus' mercy through *me*.

I am not overawed by their sins; I am struck by the fact that they have been able to recognize sins in their life that I have been blind to in my own. Hearing someone's humility breaks down my own pride. It is one of the best examinations of conscience.

Confession can actually be a scary place for a priest. Why? It is frightening because of the way in which Jesus trusts me to be a living sign of his mercy.

Archbishop Fulton Sheen once told priests that we scarcely realize what is happening when we extend our hands over someone's head in absolution. We don't realize, he said, that the very blood of Christ is dripping from our fingers onto their heads, washing the penitent clean.

The day after I was ordained, we had a little party, and my father stood up and made a toast. He has worked his entire life as an orthopedic surgeon, and he was a very good one. My whole life, his patients have come up to me at one time or another and told me how their lives have been changed because my dad was such a good surgeon.

So, there my dad was, standing in the midst of these people, and he began to say, "My whole life, I have used my hands to heal people's broken bodies. But from now on, my son Michael ... um, *Father* Michael ... will use his hands (*at this point, he got choked up*) ... he will use his hands to heal broken souls. His hands will save even more lives than mine have."

Confession is such a powerful place. All I have to do is offer God's mercy, love, and redemption ... but I don't want to get in Jesus' way. The priest stands in judgment of no one. In the confessional, the only thing I have to offer is mercy.

I GET TO SACRIFICE FOR YOU.

Lastly, when a priest hears confessions, he is taking on another responsibility.

One time, after college, I returned to confession after a long absence and a lot of sin. For a penance, the priest simply gave me something like "say one Hail Mary." I stopped.

"Um, Father ...? Did you hear everything I said?"

"Yes, I did."

"Don't you think I should get a bigger penance than that?"

He looked at me with great love and said, "No. That small penance is all that I'm asking of you." He hesitated, and then continued, "But you should know ... I will be fasting for you for the next thirty days."

I was stunned. I didn't know what to do. He told me that the *Catechism of the Catholic Church* teaches that the priest must do penance for all those who come to him for confession (see CCC 1466). And here he was, embracing a severe penance for all of my severe sins.

This is why confession reveals the priest's own soul; it reveals his willingness to sacrifice his life along with Christ. He sees our sins as a burden that he will take up (with Jesus!) and offers them to the Father, while offering us the mercy of God.

Remember, confession is always a place of victory. Whether you have confessed a particular sin for the first time, or if this is the 731st time, every confession is a win for Jesus. And I, a priest, get to be there. That's what it is like ... I get to sit and watch Jesus win his children back all day.

It is flippin' *awesome*.

WHAT'S THAT WORD?

ALLELUIA

The word *alleluia* literally means, "Praise the Lord," or, "God be praised." So when we sing (or say) "alleluia," we are praising the Lord. At Mass, outside of Lent, the Alleluia is usually sung before the Gospel reading. (During Lent, the Alleluia proclamation before the Gospel is replaced with another verse to emphasize the penitential nature of the season.)

In the Bible, the angels proclaim God's greatness, praising his name with their powerful "alleluias." (Angels were the first "music ministers," and their song of praise has been going on since God breathed them into existence.) When we proclaim "alleluia," then, we are joining in the angelic chorus.

Sometimes you will see "alleluia" spelled "hallelujah."

HOSANNA

This is a word you probably recognize from the Preface Acclamation (or *Sanctus*) at Mass, which happens right before the consecration—when we proclaim God as "Holy, holy, holy Lord, God of hosts. Heaven and earth are filled with your glory. *Hosanna* in the highest. Blessed is he who comes in the name of the Lord. *Hosanna* in the highest." You might remember, too, that the crowds greeted Jesus with "hosannas" as he entered Jerusalem on Palm Sunday (see Matthew 21:9; Mark 11:9; John 12:13).

"Hosanna" in not merely a shout of praise to God but, in its original meaning, is also a plea for his help. In Hebrew, it literally means, "Save us, we pray!" Throughout the Scriptures, "hosanna" is usually followed by a confident exclamation that God is not only aware of his people's needs but is coming to save them as well. So when we exclaim, "Hosanna in the highest" at Mass, we are crying out to God and begging him to come and save us ... from our sins, fears, anxieties ... even from *ourselves*.

"Hosanna!" is a plea of urgency for God to act; it is a call for the Lord to come and save us, but it is also a bold proclamation that God is powerful and active in our lives. We approach the Lord with humility, though, with the belief that everything will be resolved in *his* time (not ours) and that his will be done.

LITURGY

The word *liturgy* is a Greek term meaning "public work" or "work of the people"; it is something done in the service of another. The Mass is the highest form of the Church's "work," and is referred to as "the Liturgy." (Actually, the Mass itself is composed of two main parts, the "Liturgy of the Word," in which the readings and homily are proclaimed, and the "Liturgy of the Eucharist," in which the Eucharist is consecrated.) The Mass, then, is not primarily a "work" between God and the priest who is celebrating it—it is a "work" both for and with God's people. It is the "public" prayer of the Church.

So we do not just show up as individuals to hear God's Word proclaimed and receive the Eucharist—though both are indispensable to our spiritual lives. No, we come to Mass to worship God as a community, together as God's people. As Jesus himself said, "For where two or three are gathered together in my name, there am I in the midst of them" (Matthew 18:20, NAB).

At Mass, we are there for the man who just lost his wife of fifty years and for the young couple preparing to be wed. We are there for the family struggling with their son's drug addiction. We are there for the couple who desperately wants a baby but has been unable to conceive. We are there for the lonely single person who is waiting for a future spouse, for the soldier's wife who prays for his safety while he is deployed, for the baptized Catholic who wandered in after years away, and for the non-Catholic guest who is looking for "something more" and thinks that the Catholic Church might be the place to find it.

AMBO

The *ambo* (from the Greek word for "step") is the elevated platform from which the Scripture readings and homily are proclaimed during Mass. (You might also hear it referred to as the "pulpit.") In older churches built before the age of microphones and public address systems, *ambos* were very high—sometimes even reached by stairs—primarily for acoustic reasons (i.e., to help everyone in the church hear the priest's words). Today, *ambos* in modern churches tend to be lower and less ornate but remain slightly raised to symbolize the importance and centrality of Sacred Scripture in the Church's life and worship.

LECTIONARY

The *Lectionary* is the book that contains the Scripture readings for Mass. It is usually carried in the opening procession by the deacon or lector, immediately following the crucifix but before the priest. From the Latin word *lectio,* meaning "reading," the lector uses the *Lectionary* for the First and Second readings. (Some churches also use a separate *Book of the Gospels* for the Gospel proclamation, which is carried

in by the deacon. Either the priest or a deacon always proclaims the Gospel reading.)

KYRIE ELEISON ("LORD, HAVE MERCY")

In the Penitential Act at the beginning of Mass, depending on the form the priest chooses to use, we participate in a dialogue with the priest, asking for the Lord's mercy:

Priest: Lord, have mercy.
People: Lord, have mercy.
Priest: Christ, have mercy.
People: Christ, have mercy.
Priest: Lord, have mercy.
People: Lord, have mercy.

Sometimes, the original Greek form of this dialogue is used and sung as a chant: *"Kyrie eleison"* ("Lord, have mercy") and *"Christe eleison"* ("Christ, have mercy"). This prayer dates back to the very first years of the Church and was the only Greek phrase kept when the rest of the Mass began to be celebrated in Latin. (Greek was the Church's original liturgical language, as it was the most commonly spoken language of the day—much like English is today throughout the world—and was the language used in the New Testament.)

Do you want God's mercy? You should. Do you *need* God's mercy? Absolutely; everyone does. Do you *yearn* for the mercy of Christ? You ought to. We need God's mercy more than the air we breathe. The Church in its wisdom recognizes this need, and so it asks us to pause and collectively pray for God's mercy at the beginning of Mass. In this action, we acknowledge our absolute dependence on God's love, grace, and mercy, and we ask him to prepare us to hear his Word and receive him in the Eucharist.

GLORIA ("GLORY TO GOD IN THE HIGHEST")

Name the moment in the Bible when we hear these words proclaimed:

Glory to God in the highest, and on earth peace to people of good will.

If you are having trouble remembering, here is a hint: It was sung on a silent, holy night by angels, in praise of God's presence in the infant Jesus (see Luke 2:14). Shepherds were the first to enjoy this chorus, and two thousand years later, we still sing these joyful words at Mass (except during Lent).

This is appropriate, since at every Mass we celebrate Jesus' enduring presence among and within us. Jesus is *Emmanuel*, which means "God with us" (see Matthew 1:23). He has promised to remain with us always, "to the close of the age" (see Matthew 28:20). God's presence is experienced in the most profound way at Mass. The angels, too, worship with us during Mass (again, think "all things visible and *invisible*," as we proclaim in the Creed; see Colossians 1:16), singing hymns of praise to God that our earthly ears cannot hear.

FRACTION RITE

The *fraction rite* occurs as the congregation sings or recites the Lamb of God (or *Agnus Dei*). It involves the "breaking of the bread" (i.e., the Eucharist). In the fraction rite, the priest breaks off a small piece of the consecrated host and drops it into the chalice containing Christ's Precious Blood. This symbolizes that Christ's body was broken for us, and that when we receive Jesus in Communion, we become united with him and one another. As St. Paul writes, "The bread that we break, is it not a participation in the body of Christ? Because the loaf of bread is one, we, though many, are one body, for we all partake of the one loaf" (1 Corinthians 10:17, NAB).

Note, though, that in the fraction rite, Christ's Body is not just broken but united (or commingled) with his Blood. In ancient Judaism, when the priest would sacrifice the lamb in the Temple, he would drain its blood. Only when the lamb's blood was fully separated from the body was the lamb considered "dead." In the Mass, though, the sacrifice of the New Covenant, Christ's Body and Blood are not separated, signaling *death*, but united, signaling *life*. During the fraction rite, we see the fullness of life that Christ Jesus promised us all (see John 10:10).

ROMAN MISSAL

The *Roman Missal* (also known as the *Sacramentary*) is the liturgical book with the colored ribbons that contains all the prayers and blessings of the Mass—basically, all the parts of the Mass except the readings from Scripture (which are found in the *Lectionary*). It contains all the different prayers for various feasts, solemnities, and special Masses.

CIBORIUM

A *ciborium* is the gold or silver bowl that holds the Eucharistic hosts distributed at Communion. Though it sounds like something found on the Periodic Table of Elements, the word actually comes from the Latin *cibus* meaning "food." You may see the priest or deacon place the *ciboria* (the plural of *ciborium*) in the tabernacle after Communion.

"ENTER UNDER MY ROOF"

What may sound like one of the strangest prayers we utter at Mass is actually, Scripturally speaking, one of the most human and most beautiful:

Lord, I am not worthy that you should enter under my roof, but only say the word and my soul shall be healed.

This prayer comes from the well-known scene in the Gospel where Jesus is approached by a centurion whose servant is paralyzed:

> As he entered Capernaum, a centurion came forward to him, begging him and saying, "Lord, my servant is lying paralyzed at home, in terrible distress." And he said to him, "I will come and heal him." But the centurion answered him, "Lord, I am not worthy to have you come under my roof; but only say the word, and my servant will be healed" (Matthew 8:5-8; also check out the entire story in Matthew 8:5-13).

Remember that Jews and Gentiles did not interact with one another for the most part, which is one of the reasons Jesus was constantly getting into so much trouble with the religious authorities of his day.

Picture the scene. A Roman centurion was a high-ranking officer who commanded at least a hundred men, yet here he was publicly affirming Jesus' identity and begging him for help to heal his servant. The idea of a Jewish rabbi going to the home of a Gentile military officer would have shocked and scandalized nearly everyone. The centurion exercised great authority, which is another reason that his proclamation of Jesus' authority to heal his servant is so impressive (see Matthew 8:9). In addition, the centurion acknowledges his unworthiness for Jesus to enter his house—in the same way we acknowledge in Mass our unworthiness for Christ to enter under the "roof" of our souls in Holy Communion. But just as the centurion believed Christ could heal his servant, we as Christ's servants believe he can and will heal us of our unworthiness to receive him in the Eucharist.

St. Paul reminds us that our bodies are "temples of the Holy Spirit" (see 1 Corinthians 6:19). When we receive Jesus Christ in the Eucharist, he is literally coming under the "roof" of our "temples." He is the sacrifice upon the altar of our temples (our hearts). As Jesus enters under our roof, he transforms us into living, walking tabernacles to be sent out into the world. As the *Catechism* reminds us, "Before so great a sacrament, the faithful can only echo humbly and with ardent faith the words of the centurion" (CCC 1386).

It might initially feel strange to pray "under my roof" when speaking about our own bodily temples, but this is an opportunity to pray in a more contemplative way. Place yourself within the scene you read about in the Gospel. Feel the humidity in the air and the dirt beneath your feet. Listen to the humble boldness of the centurion's words and the joyful response such humility evokes in the heart of Jesus. Hold on to that image when you pray these words with your whole heart:

Lord, I am not worthy that you should enter under my roof, but only say the word and my soul shall be healed.

The more you learn about the "ins and outs" of the Mass, the more it will come to life for you. Knowing what is happening sacramentally might not change your life, but contemplating the prayers being offered within it can. Noticing the washing at the *lavabo* can not only act as a mental invitation to reengage a wandering mind but also can serve as an opportunity to pray for all of Christ's priests in gratitude for their service and sacrifice to make the Lord available to us on altars around the world.

Remember, the Creator can use all created things to point our minds and hearts back to him.

Resources for Diving in Deeper

Introduction

When God speaks, things happen.

God spoke, and there was light. God spoke, and there was sea and sky, land and plants, animals and man. In the Gospels, when Christ spoke, mighty winds ceased, plants withered, demons were driven out, people came back to life, and sins were forgiven.

When God speaks—even if his people do not listen—things *always* happen.

So, when Christ took bread and wine into his hands and proclaimed it his Body and his Blood, *something extraordinary happened.* In the same way, through the power of the Holy Spirit, every time a priest takes bread and wine and speaks the words of consecration in the Eucharistic Prayer at Mass, *something extraordinary happens.* What still looks and tastes like bread and wine has now become the very Body and Blood of Christ. The Eucharist, then, is not merely a *symbol* of Christ's Body and Blood; it is his very Body, Blood, Soul, and Divinity.

As we have seen, the Church refers to this miraculous change as "transubstantiation." You may remember that this means that the bread and wine are changed on the level of substance into Christ's true Body and Blood— though they continue to appear as bread and wine. While this is a difficult concept to understand, the *Catechism* reminds us that the Eucharist is the "source and summit" of our faith (CCC 1324), which means that everything we *are* and everything we *do* as a Church flows from the Eucharist (its source) and moves us toward the Eucharist (its summit). On the most

fundamental level, then, the Eucharist is what it means to be Catholic.

Christ's real presence in the Eucharist is simultaneously one of the most profound mysteries and one of the greatest gifts of our Catholic Faith. Saints and scholars have spent their entire lives meditating upon this truth. Libraries could be filled with the books and treatises on the Eucharist. So we can only give you some suggestions, insights, explanations, and tools for you to use the next time you are in Christ's true presence—before the Eucharist—in Adoration of the Blessed Sacrament.

Typically, an appendix is a collection of additional information that is looked at or used by relatively few readers. The elements contained here, however, have the power to transform not only your experience of the Mass but also your entire life. The more you "put out into the deep" at Mass, the more you will come to know God and to learn the unique vocation he has designed for you.

Ask the Holy Spirit to open your mind and heart to the Lord as you read the following sections. Ask the Lord to give you eyes of faith so you can see what so many saints before you have seen in the Eucharist.

At the Last Supper, Jesus said, "This is my body" (Matthew 26:26). Before his ascension, Jesus told his apostles, "I am with you always" (Matthew 28:20). You can take Jesus at his word; you can trust him. Allow Jesus to love you through the Mass and throughout this study. Allow him to speak to your soul now—because when God speaks ... *things happen.*

The Order of the Mass

As we saw earlier, the Mass is one Liturgy composed of two main components: the Liturgy of the Word and the Liturgy of the Eucharist. There are several pieces and parts, as well as particular movements and moments, within both liturgies. The better you begin to understand the "Order" of the Mass and its "flow," the more sense it will make to you.

In addition to the Liturgy of the Word and the Liturgy of the Eucharist, the Mass also has Introductory Rites at the beginning, which help us to enter into the solemn mysteries we are about to celebrate, and Concluding Rites after Communion, which send us out with the blessing of the Church to serve God and one another.

Here is an overview of the Order of the Mass:

Introductory Rites	Liturgy of the Word	Liturgy of the Eucharist	Concluding Rites
• Entrance song and procession	• First Reading (from the Old Testament except during Easter, when it is from the New Testament)	• Presentation of the Gifts and Preparation of the Altar	• Final Blessing
• Sign of the Cross		• Prayer Over the Offerings	• Dismissal
• Penitential Act (*Kyrie eleison* or "Lord, have mercy")	• Responsorial Psalm	• Eucharistic Prayer	
• *Gloria* ("Glory to God") – *on Sundays, solemnities, and feasts*	• Second Reading (from a New Testament letter) – on Sundays and solemnities	– Preface	
		– *Sanctus* ("Holy, Holy, Holy")	
• Collect (or Opening Prayer)	• Gospel Acclamation (Alleluia, except during Lent)	– *Epiclesis*	
		– Institution Narrative/ Consecration	
	• Homily	– Mystery of Faith (or *Anamnesis*)	
	• Profession of Faith (Nicene Creed) – on Sundays, solemnities, and special occasions	– Oblation	
		– Intercessions	
	• Universal Prayer (or Prayer of the Faithful)	– Doxology ("Through him, with him, in him")	
		• Communion Rite	
		– Our Father (the Lord's Prayer)	
		– Sign of Peace	
		– Fraction Rite ("Lamb of God")	
		– Communion	
		– Prayer after Communion	

Altar Servers 101:
An Introduction to "Holy" Stuff

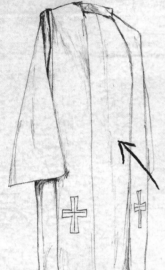

Alb (from the Latin *albus*, meaning "white") – the white robe the priest wears underneath his outer vestment (see "Chasuble"). It is a symbol of baptism and was typically worn by adult catechumens when they were baptized by immersion in the early centuries of the Church. The white garment placed on infants today during baptism flows from this earlier tradition. You will usually see a deacon assisting at Mass wearing an alb with a stole (see "Stole") worn diagonally across his body.

Ambo (from the Greek word for "step") – the elevated platform (or lectern) from which the Scripture readings and homily are proclaimed.

Book of the Gospels – the usually decorated and oversized liturgical book that contains the Gospel readings for Mass. It is typically carried by the deacon in the opening procession.

Ciborium (from the Latin *cibus*, meaning "food") – the bowl that holds the consecrated hosts used during the distribution of the Eucharist at Mass. Hosts not consumed during Mass are reserved in *ciboria* (the plural of *ciborium*) in the tabernacle for veneration and distribution of Communion to the sick.

Chalice (from the Latin *calix*, meaning "cup") – the sacred vessel, usually made of precious metal, which holds the consecrated wine, the Lord's most Precious Blood.

Chasuble (from the Latin for "hooded cloak") – the colored, outer vestment the priest wears over his alb and stole (see "Stole"). The chasuble is sleeveless, and its color varies according to the liturgical season or feast day. The chasuble is a symbol of the priest's charity, as well as of the authority he has acting *in persona Christi* ("in the person of Christ") as celebrant of the Mass.

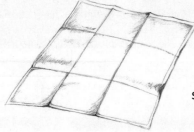

Corporal (from the Latin *corpus*, meaning "body") – the thin white linen cloth that is unfolded and placed upon the altar on which the sacred vessels are placed.

Lectionary (from the Latin *lectio*, meaning "reading") – the official liturgical book that contain the Scripture readings for Mass. If the Book of the Gospels is not used, the lector or deacon carries the *Lectionary* in the opening procession.

Monstrance (from a Latin word meaning "to show forth") – the sacred vessel that holds and displays the Eucharistic host during Adoration. Monstrances are traditionally made of precious metal and have an ornate design (though you may occasionally see a wooden monstrance used as well).

Pall (from the Latin *pallium,* meaning "covering" or "cloak") – the square, white cover that is placed over the chalice. It symbolizes Christ's burial cloth and his victory over death in his passion, death, and resurrection. Its practical purpose—believe it or not—is to keep dust and insects from falling into the Precious Blood.

Paten (from the Latin *patina,* meaning "pan" or "shallow plate") – the round plate, made of gold or silver, that holds the bread that becomes Christ's Body in the Eucharist.

Purificator – the white cloth used by a priest or extraordinary minister of the Eucharist to wipe the chalice after people receive from the cup at Communion.

Roman Missal – the official liturgical book used by the priest (and deacon) that contains all the elements of the Mass except the Scripture readings (which are found in the *Lectionary*). This includes the opening and closing prayers, prefaces, Eucharistic Prayers, and blessings. (Also known as the *Sacramentary*.)

Sanctuary Lamp – a large candle placed near the tabernacle (see "Tabernacle") that always remains lit to remind us of Christ's abiding presence in the Eucharist.

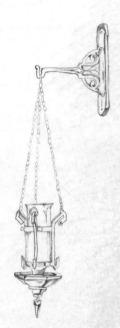

Stole – the long, narrow strip of colored fabric worn by a priest around his neck with the ends hanging down in front. It symbolizes his priestly authority. A deacon also wears a stole, but his is placed over his left shoulder, and it lays diagonally over his chest, secured on his right side. It symbolizes that he shares in the sacrament of holy orders. As with the chasuble, the color of the stole reflects the liturgical season or feast day.

Tabernacle (from the Latin *tabernaculum*, meaning "tent" or "hut") – the fixed, locked box, usually behind the altar or in a side chapel, where the consecrated Eucharistic hosts are reserved.

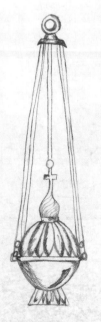

Thurible (from the Latin *thus*, meaning "incense"; also called a "censer") – the metal holder in which incense is burned during Mass. It is typically carried in the entrance procession and used to incense the cross and the altar at the beginning of Mass. It is then used to incense the Gospel prior to it being proclaimed, the gifts offered on the altar, the elevation of the consecrated host, and the priest (usually by a deacon) and the congregation.

Finding the Mass Prayers in Scripture

Some non-Catholics have claimed that the Mass is not "biblical." In reality, the *entire* Mass is rooted in Sacred Scripture. The next time you attend Mass, listen for the following prayers, all of which are directly from the Bible:

- "In the name of the Father and of the Son and of the Holy Spirit" **(Matthew 28:19)**.

- "Amen" **(found throughout the Old and New Testaments)**.

- "The grace of our Lord Jesus Christ, the love of God, and the fellowship of the Holy Spirit be with you" **(2 Corinthians 13:13, NAB)**.

- "The Lord be with you" **(Ruth 2:4; 2 Chronicles 15:2; Numbers 14:42)**.

- "Glory to God in the highest and peace on Earth to people of good will" **(see Luke 2:14)**.

- "Blessed be God forever" **(see Psalm 68:36)**.

- "May the Lord accept the sacrifice at your hands" **(see Psalm 50:23)**.

- "Lift up your hearts ... we lift them up to the Lord" **(see Lamentations 3:41)**.

- "Let us give thanks to the Lord our God" **(see Colossians 3:17)**.

- "Holy, holy, holy [is the] LORD, God of hosts" **(Isaiah 6:3)**.

- "Hosanna in the highest, blessed is he who comes in the name of the Lord" **(Matthew 21:9)**.

- "Lord, you are holy indeed, the fountain of all holiness" **(see 2 Maccabees 14:36)**.

- "You never cease to gather a people to yourself, so that from the rising of the sun to its setting" **(Psalm 113:3)**.

- "Through him, and with him, and in him" **(see Romans 11:36)**.

- "Behold, the Lamb of God. Behold him who takes away the sins of the world. Blessed are those called to the supper of the Lamb" **(see John 1:29; Revelation 19:9)**.

Tips for Getting More Out of Mass

1. Get the "lay of the liturgical land."

In other words, get to know the Catholic community that is your parish. Stop by your parish church when Mass is not being celebrated. Slowly and prayerfully take in every element of the church. Contemplate the crucifix. Look closely at the stained glass windows. Stop to appreciate every statue. Approach the sanctuary and kneel at the altar rail, taking in all the sacred architecture. Pause at the baptismal font and thank God for the gift of your own baptism. Kneel in humble appreciation for the Lord's perpetual Eucharistic presence, symbolized by the sanctuary lamp burning brightly beside the tabernacle. The more intentionally you "see" the church's environment (and understand what each element signifies), the more deeply you will be able to enter into the Mass with your mind and heart.

2. Read the Scripture readings *before* Mass.

Read all four readings—the First Reading, the Responsorial Psalm, the Second Reading, and the Gospel—ahead of time. (They can be found at usccb.org/bible—the official website of the United States Conference of Catholic Bishops. Just click on the calendar for the upcoming Sunday, and the readings will come up.) Read all four on Monday and then again over the course of the week (or read one reading each day). If possible, get a good Bible commentary and see what it says for each reading. This will help draw you more deeply into the context and meaning of the reading. Take advantage of free audio and video podcasts that are available. That way, if a baby cries or your mind wanders, you need not worry; you will have already read and studied the day's Scripture and will understand what is being proclaimed.

3. Pack your bags.

Many people claim they don't "get anything out of" Mass, but maybe this is because they fail to bring anything to it. God wants us to bring our issues, stresses, anxieties, fears, and concerns—our personal "baggage"—with us to Mass. So check your "bags" at the altar. Bring a special intention with you, someone or something you want to offer up to the Lord upon the altar alongside the gifts. Remember that at Mass, Jesus offers up his very life for you. Are you willing to offer up to him those things that may keep you from following and loving him more perfectly?

4. Get wet.

Dipping your fingers into the holy water when you enter and leave the church can become just a habit. Make this profound gesture intentional. As you reach toward the font, thank God for the gift of your baptism, by which you became God's son or daughter and entered the life of faith. As you trace the Sign of the Cross on your body, contemplate how water brings both life and death, and consider how important it is to be filled with God's grace through the sacraments.

5. Sit up.

That is, sit up closer—to the front. Why is it that people want front-row seats at concerts and sporting events but prefer sitting in the back row at Mass? The closer you are to the sanctuary, the better view you will have to witness heaven visit earth through the power of the Holy Spirit. While you are at it, do not just sit closer to the front, but change seats frequently. Many Catholics seem to gravitate toward the same seats or have "their pew." Changing seats gives you a different perspective and may help you get to know other parishioners in your community of faith.

6. Strike a chord with God.

While many Catholics may open the hymnal at Mass, too many take the word "refrain" literally—as in, they *refrain* (keep) from singing! If God gave you a beautiful voice, then praise him with it. If God gave you a horrible voice, sing anyway. Remember that singing at Mass lifts your voice, mind, and heart to your heavenly Father. St. Augustine said that when we sing, we pray twice. "Set the tone" for others through your example. The Mass, of course, is more than music, and many parishes could undoubtedly "do music" better, but you can help improve it by participating. If you sing well or play an instrument, consider joining the choir or music ministry.

7. Go through with your "heart transplant."

Are you really offering your heart upon the altar along with the gifts of bread and wine? Are you giving God permission to have his way with your life, entrusting him with your entire life now and your future? Do you pray like Christ on his knees in the Garden of Gethsemane, asking that the Father's will be done, or are you one of the disciples who falls asleep? At Mass, Christ is offering you redemption, a time to exchange your tired, sin-tattered heart for his exuberant, Sacred Heart. Take him up on his offer. Give God permission to transform your heart along with the gifts offered upon the altar.

8. Say it like you mean it.

Extend a hand during the Sign of Peace to those around you as though it were your last chance to right a wrong. Offer genuine forgiveness to any family members or friends who have wronged you, and humbly seek the forgiveness of others. This is a great warm-up for heaven. It is for the dads who yelled in the car on their way to Mass and the moms who ran out of patience an hour before the opening prayer. This is for the kids who talked back that morning and the friend who upset you greatly the night before. The Sign of Peace is not just a time to "get right" with one another but also an opportunity to give others permission to hold you to a higher standard. It demonstrates your humility as well as God's grace actively at work in you.

9. Relish the silence.

Relish the silent moments at Mass. Silence, properly understood, is God's gift to us. It gives us an opportunity, like the Beloved Disciple at the Last Supper, to draw near to Jesus and rest our heads upon his chest. The Mass' silent breaks are chances to "get quiet" with God, to take a break from all the noise and distractions of our media- and electronics-filled lives. The saints remind us that it is in these moments that we can be closest to God.

10. Go forth with purpose.

Do you leave Mass with a mission? There are people who desperately need what you have! Before you exit the pew and genuflect, have a purpose and a plan. Who are you going to invite to Mass next Sunday? Who are you going to reach out to at work or school? What areas of your life do you need to work on? How can you unleash the gift of grace within your soul you have just received in the Eucharist over the coming week? The question is not whether you have been empowered at Mass but whether you comprehend the power that exists within you—and what you plan to do about it.

Battling Through Distractions

What if my mind wanders at Mass? What can I do?

We all get distracted at times. We live in a loud and busy culture. Our lives are filled with endless motion and different kinds of noise. Smart phones, iPads, and many other electronic devices demand our attention. Sitting in silence can be challenging, especially when you are not used to it.

You might feel your mind wander at Mass or in Eucharistic Adoration. You might be paying attention to everything *but* Jesus. Don't be too hard on yourself. It is normal to get distracted from time to time; it is part of our fallen nature. (It is also part of the devil's strategy to keep us from praying, to keep us from drawing near to Jesus and hearing him speak to us in our hearts.)

Four things to do when you find yourself distracted during Mass (or during prayer in general):

1. **Consider your posture and surroundings.** Are the distractions due to where you are sitting or who you are sitting next to? Can you find a different spot in the church that might allow you to enter into the prayer more deeply—maybe closer to the front of church, nearer to the altar? What is your posture? Are you sitting up straight? Are you more engaged when you kneel?

   Sometimes a shift in your posture can make the big difference in your ability to focus your attention.

2. **Think about your responses.** Pay attention to the words you are saying. Offer true responses of praise and blessing. Consider the words you are singing. Words do matter—in life and especially at Mass and in prayer.

3. **Offer up your distractions for God's glory.** If you really are trying to sing, respond, and pray but are still distracted, offer up your distracting thoughts to God. Say a simple prayer like, "God, I offer up these distracting thoughts to you for your glory." If the distracting thoughts are from the devil, then they will usually stop, as he does not want to us to do anything that gives God glory. If they persist, it may mean that this is a struggle that God wants you to bring to him. Spend some focused time praying about this challenge, and be sure to let God do most of the talking.

4. **Bring your Bible.** Bookmark the Mass readings ahead of time in your Bible. Follow along as the readings are proclaimed during the Liturgy of the Word.

   At Eucharistic Adoration, you may want to bring a journal in which you can record the things swimming around in your brain that are keeping you from praying. Sometimes getting them on paper is the best way of clearing your head so you can be fully present.

Quotes About the Eucharist

"[Holy Communion] is our daily bread; take it daily, that it may profit you daily. Live, as to deserve to receive it daily." – *St. Augustine*

"Holy Communion is the shortest and safest way to heaven." – *St. Pius X*

"The Holy Eucharist is the perfect expression of the love of Jesus Christ for man." – *St. Maria Goretti*

"They abstain from the Eucharist because they do not confess that the Eucharist is the flesh of our Savior Jesus Christ, flesh which suffered for our sins and which that Father, in his goodness, raised up again. They who deny the gift of God are perishing in their disputes." – *St. Ignatius of Antioch*

"As in the life of the body, after a man is born and becomes strong, he requires food that his life may be preserved and sustained; so also in the spiritual life, after being fortified, he requires spiritual food, which is Christ's Body: 'Unless you shall eat of the flesh of the Son of Man, and drink of his blood, you shall not have life in you.'" – *St. Thomas Aquinas*

"Without the Holy Eucharist there would be no happiness in this world; life would be insupportable." – *St. John Vianney*

"Yesterday, as I drew near to Jesus in the Most Blessed Sacrament, I felt myself burning so violently, that I was obliged to move away. I was burning all over; it rose even to my face. Blessed be Jesus! How does it happen that so many who are standing so close to Jesus do not burn to ashes?" – *St. Gemma Galgani*

"Do you think that this most holy food isn't nourishment for these bodies and an excellent remedy even against bodily ailments? ... If when he lived in this world, he healed the sick by the mere touch of his garments, what doubt is there but that he will perform miracles, since he is so intimately within us, if we have a lively faith; and that he will grant us what we ask of him, while he is in our house?" – *St. Teresa of Avila*

"When Our Lord sees pure souls coming eagerly to visit him in the Blessed Sacrament, he smiles on them." – *St. John Vianney*

"Do not, therefore, regard the bread and wine as simply that, for they are, according to the Master's declaration, the Body and Blood of Christ. Even though the senses suggest to you the other, let faith make you firm." – *St. Cyril of Jerusalem*

"Let us return from that Table like lions breathing out fire, terrifying to the devil!" – *St. John Chrysostom*

"Every day [Jesus] humbles himself just as he did when he came from his *heavenly throne*[1] into the Virgin's womb; every day, he comes to us and lets us see him in [lowliness], when he descends from the bosom of the Father into the hands of the priest at the altar." – *St. Francis of Assisi*

"Jesus Christ said over the consecrated elements, 'This is my body.' You say, 'No. It is not his body.' Whom am I to believe? I prefer to believe Jesus Christ." – *Blessed Dominic Barberi*

"Our way of thinking is attuned to the Eucharist, and the Eucharist in turn confirms our way of thinking." – *Catechism of the Catholic Church 1327*[2]

"And lo, I am with you always, to the close of the age." – *Matthew 28:20*

"This is my body." – *Mark 14:22*

"They told what had happened on the road, and how he was known to them in the breaking of the bread." – *Luke 24:35*

"If any one eats of this bread, he will live for ever; and the bread which I shall give for the life of the world is my flesh." – *John 6:51*

"They devoted themselves to the apostles' teaching and fellowship, to the breaking of bread and the prayers." – *Acts 2:42*

"For as often as you eat this bread and drink the cup, you proclaim the Lord's death until he comes." – *1 Corinthians 11:26*

---

[1]   Wisdom 18:15.
[2]   St. Irenaeus, *Adv. Haereses.* 4, 18, 5: PG 7/1, 1028.

Prayers You Might Hear During (and After) Mass

Confiteor ("I Confess")

I confess to almighty God and to you, my brothers and sisters, that I have greatly sinned, in my thoughts and in my words, in what I have done and in what I have failed to do, *(All strike their breast three times during the following two lines)* through my fault, through my fault, through my most grievous fault; therefore I ask blessed Mary ever-Virgin, all the angels and saints, and you, my brothers and sisters, to pray for me to the Lord our God.

Gloria ("Glory to God in the Highest")

Glory to God in the highest, and on earth peace to people of good will.

We praise you, we bless you, we adore you, we glorify you, we give you thanks for your great glory, Lord God, heavenly King, O God, almighty Father.

Lord Jesus Christ, Only Begotten Son, Lord God, Lamb of God, Son of the Father, you take away the sins of the world, have mercy on us; you take away the sins of the world, receive our prayer; you are seated at the right hand of the Father, have mercy on us.

For you alone are the Holy One, you alone are the Lord, you alone are the Most High, Jesus Christ, with the Holy Spirit, in the glory of God the Father. Amen.

Nicene Creed

I believe in one God, the Father almighty, maker of heaven and earth, of all things visible and invisible.

I believe in one Lord Jesus Christ, the Only Begotten Son of God, born of the Father before all ages. God from God, Light from Light, true God from true God, begotten, not made, consubstantial with the Father; through him all things were made. For us men and for our salvation he came down from heaven, and by the Holy Spirit was incarnate of the Virgin Mary, and became man.

For our sake he was crucified under Pontius Pilate, he suffered death and was buried, and rose again on the third day in accordance with the Scriptures. He ascended into heaven and is seated at the right hand of the Father. He will come again in glory to judge the living and the dead and his kingdom will have no end.

I believe in the Holy Spirit, the Lord, the giver of life, who proceeds from the Father and the Son, who with the Father and the Son is adored and glorified, who has spoken through the prophets.

I believe in one, holy, catholic and apostolic Church. I confess one Baptism for the forgiveness of sins and I look forward to the resurrection of the dead and the life of the world to come. Amen.

The Our Father (or Lord's Prayer)

Our Father, who art in heaven, hallowed be thy name. Thy kingdom come. Thy will be done on earth as it is in heaven.

Give us this day our daily bread, and forgive us our trespasses, as we forgive those who trespass against us; and lead us not into temptation, but deliver us from evil. Amen.

Prayer of Thanksgiving (St. Thomas Aquinas) – prayed after Mass

Lord, Father all-powerful and ever-living God, I thank you, for even though I am a sinner, your unprofitable servant, not because of my worth but in the kindness of your mercy, you have fed me with the Precious Body and Blood of your Son, our Lord Jesus Christ.

I pray that this Holy Communion may not bring me condemnation and punishment but forgiveness and salvation.

May it be a helmet of faith and a shield of good will. May it purify me from evil ways and put an end to my evil passions. May it bring me charity and patience, humility and obedience, and growth in the power to do good.

May it be my strong defense against all my enemies, visible and invisible, and the perfect calming of all my evil impulses, bodily and spiritual.

May it unite me more closely to you, the One true God, and lead me safely through death to everlasting happiness with you.

And I pray that you will lead me, a sinner, to the banquet where you, with your Son and Holy Spirit, are true and perfect light, total fulfillment, everlasting joy, gladness without end, and perfect happiness to your saints. Grant this through Christ our Lord. Amen.

Prayers for Eucharistic Adoration and Benediction

LATIN	ENGLISH
O Salutaris Hostia	"O Saving Victim"
O Salutaris Hostia Quae caeli pandis ostium. Bella premunt hostilia; Da robur, fer auxilium. Uni trinoque Domino Sit sempiterna gloria: Qui vitam sine termino, Nobis donet in patria. Amen.	O Saving Victim opening wide The gate of heaven to all below. Our foes press on from every side; Thine aid supply, thy strength bestow. To thy great name be endless praise Immortal Godhead, One in Three; Oh, grant us endless length of days, In our true native land with thee. Amen.
Tantum Ergo	"Down in Adoration Falling"
Tantum ergo Sacramentum Veneremur cernui: Et antiquum documentum Novo cedat ritui: Praestet fides supplementum Sensuum defectui. Genitori, Genitoque Laus et iubilatio, Salus, honor, virtus quoque Sit et benedictio: Procedenti ab utroque Compar sit laudatio. Amen. **V.** Panem de caelo praestitisti eis. **R.** Omne delectamentum in se habentem. Oremus: Deus, qui nobis sub sacramento mirabili, passionis tuae memoriam reliquisti: tribue, quaesumus, ita nos corporis et sanguinis tui sacra mysteria venerari, ut redemptionis tuae fructum in nobis iugiter sentiamus. Qui vivis et regnas in saecula saeculorum. **R.** Amen.	Down in adoration falling, Lo! the sacred Host we hail, Lo! oe'r ancient forms departing Newer rites of grace prevail; Faith for all defects supplying, Where the feeble senses fail. To the everlasting Father, And the Son who reigns on high With the Holy Spirit proceeding Forth from each eternally, Be salvation, honor blessing, Might and endless majesty. Amen. **V.** Thou hast given them bread from heaven. **R.** Having within it all sweetness. Let us pray: O God, who in this wonderful Sacrament left us a memorial of thy Passion: Grant, we implore thee, that we may so venerate the sacred mysteries of thy Body and Blood, as always to be conscious of the fruit of thy Redemption. Thou who livest and reignest forever and ever. **R.** Amen.

Divine Praises

Blessed be God.

Blessed be his Holy Name.

Blessed be Jesus Christ, true God and true man.

Blessed be the name of Jesus.

Blessed be his Most Sacred Heart.

Blessed be his Most Precious Blood.

Blessed be Jesus in the Most Holy Sacrament of the Altar.

Blessed be the Holy Spirit the Paraclete.

Blessed be the great Mother of God, Mary Most Holy.

Blessed be her holy and Immaculate Conception.

Blessed be her glorious Assumption.

Blessed be the name of Mary, Virgin and Mother.

Blessed be St. Joseph, her most chaste spouse.

Blessed be God in his angels and in his saints.

Amen.

Think Before You Pray

Additional Words and Phrases You Will Hear at Mass and Need to Understand

What words have you said in the past hour? The past day? We say lots of words, usually without thinking too much about them. But words are powerful, especially words used to express our belief in God and to communicate with him. The words we speak and hear at Mass are "massively" important.

This section will unpack some of the words and phrases you hear at Mass. Some of them will be familiar, while others will be foreign. But all of them are important. Through the words we pray at Mass, we connect with God, who seeks to be connected with us. At every Mass, the God of the universe makes himself fully present to us. Through the words we pray, we respond to him. Mass is *way* too important to say words we do not understand. When we take the time to understand the words we say, our prayer takes on greater depth and meaning.

So take your time with the pages that follow. Use it as a guide and come back to it often. The Mass is like an iceberg—ninety percent of its depth lies beneath the surface. The more you learn about the Mass, the more you will want to learn, and that is a great problem to have.

1. Contrite

As a child, did you ever say "sorry" to a brother or sister because your mother or father made you? Think back to a time when you got into trouble. Maybe you hit your brother, sister, or friend or refused to share with them. In an effort to teach you right from wrong, your parents forced you to look your sibling or friend in the eyes and apologize for your actions. You most likely apologized out of fear of punishment but without any true sorrow for what you did.

As we grow older, we (hopefully) become more mature as Christians. If we wrong our brothers and sisters—and especially if we wrong our heavenly Father—we do not just *say*, "I'm sorry," but we sincerely *mean* it.

This is why the words "contrite" and "contrition" are so important. "Contrite" comes from a Latin word meaning "to rub together" or "to grind down." It describes how our sincere and heartfelt sorrow for a sinful thought or action

"grinds down" our pride and wears away our self-centeredness. When we are truly contrite we have a firm resolution to try our best not to sin again. Being contrite means adding, "and with God's help, I vow not to do it again," to our, "I'm sorry."

Some people are sorry for their sinful actions only out of fear of punishment. This is known as "attrition." True contrition, though, is an acknowledgment that God calls us to something more, to become better and grow in our relationship with him every day. We are a work in progress, and being contrite for our failings is essential if we want to become what God has designed us to be (see Ephesians 2:10). We are desperately in need of his help and his grace.

This is why, during the sacrament of reconciliation, we pray an Act of Contrition right before the priest gives us absolution. The Act of Contrition is not just "part of the formula" of the sacrament; it is an opportunity for us to express our sorrow for our sins—and mean it. It is our prayer to God, humbly asking him for his forgiveness and promising him that we will try to avoid sin in the future.

If we love God above all else and above everyone else, our greatest sadness should be that when we sin, we damage our relationship with him. If we are truly contrite and confess our sins in the sacrament of reconciliation, though, our relationship with God will be restored and strengthened. We will begin to overcome certain sins and grow in holiness every day.

2. Only Begotten

She's my girl.
He's like the son I never had.
My brother from another mother.

Such phrases are used to express the importance of a friendship or relationship with someone to whom we are not related. Just saying, "He's my friend," or, "He matters to me," is not enough, so we try to find a way to express the depth of our relationship with that person.

During Mass, most specifically in the *Gloria*, the Creed, and the Eucharistic Prayer, instead of simply saying "the Son of God," the Church refers to Jesus Christ as the "Only *Begotten* Son" (see John 1:14, 3:16). As Christians, we believe that Jesus was not *created* by the Father in the same way a child is created by his or her parents. Instead, Jesus was begotten, which means that he always was—he has existed as the Second Person of the Trinity from all eternity. (The word "begotten" literally means "generated from" or "flowing from.") As the psalmist says in

foretelling the coming of the Messiah: "You are my son, today I have begotten you" (Psalm 2:7).

God the Father is the eternal lamp that "begets" the "light of the world," Jesus (see John 8:12). As we proclaim in the Creed, Jesus was "begotten, not made," which indicates his eternal divine nature. Though he became incarnate at an appointed moment in history, taking on a human nature, there was never a time when Jesus "was not." Jesus is "the eternal Word of God" (John 1:1-5); always has been, always will be.

The use of "Only Begotten" in reference to Jesus draws a clear distinction between him and us. He is the only "natural" Son of God, sharing in the divine nature from all eternity. You and I, though, are God's sons and daughters only through baptism, which brought us into a relationship with him through grace. As St. Paul tells us, we have "received a spirit of adoption, through which we cry, 'Abba, Father!'" (Romans, 8:15, NAB).

3. Alleluia

What is the first thing you think of when you hear the word "alleluia"?

The word "alleluia" literally means, "Praise the Lord" or "God be praised." So when we sing (or say) "alleluia," we are praising the Lord. At Mass (outside of Lent), the Alleluia is usually sung

before the Gospel reading. (During Lent, to emphasize the penitential nature of the season, the Alleluia proclamation before the Gospel is replaced with another verse.)

You may think of it as the signal to stand before the Gospel reading, as a sort of a "conditioned response" you learn after going to Mass for many years. Or it might bring to mind a time during Lent when you were not supposed to say the "A" word and did, by accident. Since we say it so frequently, however, and intentionally "avoid" saying it for an entire season of the Church's year, that should be a signal to us that it is an important prayer within the Mass.

In the Bible, the angels proclaim God's greatness, praising his name with their powerful "alleluias." (Angels are the first "music ministers," and their song of praise has been going on since God breathed them into existence.) When we proclaim "alleluia," then, we are joining in the angelic chorus.

4. Incarnate

As Christians, we acknowledge the birth of Jesus each year on Christmas. But there is something more at work here, a much deeper truth.

Nine months before Christmas, on March 25th, the Church celebrates the Annunciation of the Lord, when Mary's "yes" to the words of the archangel Gabriel made her the mother of Jesus and the Mother of God (see Luke 1:38). From that moment, we believe that the Second Person of the Trinity, the Son of God, "was incarnate" in Mary's womb.

As an eternal divine person, the Son of God has always existed. He is "consubstantial" with (i.e., a philosophical term meaning "of the same substance as") God the Father. At a specific moment in history, just over two thousand years ago, he took on a true human nature and was born of Mary. He became like us in everything but sin. When he took on our flesh, Jesus also took on our sufferings (see Hebrews 5:7).

So why did God become man? Why did the "Word become flesh"?

The Nicene Creed, which we pray every Sunday at Mass, gives us the answer: "Through him [Jesus] all things were made. For us men and

for *our salvation*, he came down from heaven" (emphasis added).

St. Paul explained the profound mystery of the Incarnation to the Christians in Philippi in these words:

> Christ Jesus, who, though he was in the form of God, did not count equality with God a thing to be grasped, but emptied himself, taking the form of a servant, being born in the likeness of men. And being found in human form he humbled himself and became obedient unto death, even death on a cross (Philippians 2:5-8).

These words contain very deep truths. God took on human flesh. He became what we are to give us what he is; he came down to us from heaven so that we could go from earth to heaven with him. Through the Incarnation, God meets us "where we are at," walking and pointing us to where he wants us to go.

The eternal Son of God, then, came down from heaven and became man to save us. Save us from what? From our sins, so that we can live a life in friendship with God on earth and have a relationship with him in heaven forever.

5. *Sanctus, Sanctus, Sanctus* ("Holy, Holy, Holy")

You know these words. You have sung (or said) them at every Mass. After the Preface of the Eucharistic Prayer, before the consecration, we proclaim:

Holy, Holy, Holy Lord God of hosts.
Heaven and earth are full of your glory.
Hosanna in the highest.
Blessed is he who comes in the name of the Lord.
Hosanna in the highest.

It may also be sung in its original Latin form:

Sanctus, Sanctus, Sanctus Dominus Deus
sabbaoth.
Pleni sunt caeli et terra gloria tua.
Hosanna in excelsis.
Benedictus qui venit in nomine Domini.
Hosanna in excelsis.

The exclamation "holy, holy, holy" is found in Scripture in Isaiah 6:1-5 and Revelation 4:2-8.

Both passages unveil images of God's heavenly throne room and the unceasing worship there.

When we sing the *Sanctus* ("Holy, Holy, Holy"), we are joining into the song of the angels and saints in heaven. It is a humble acknowledgment of God's majesty and a song of praise. The *Sanctus* is a celebration of God's presence among us. Just as in the passages from Isaiah and Revelation mentioned earlier (which you should read on your own), we ought to be filled with an earth-shattering, soul-stirring awe that God would make his presence known to us in the Mass.

Try to learn the Latin version of the *Sanctus*, as well as the Latin version of the *Tantum Ergo* (see page 92). This is a fun way to connect with the heritage of the Church, to broaden your prayer life, and to pray with Catholics of other countries using our common liturgical language ... and it makes you sound really smart.

6. God of Hosts

The phrase "God of hosts" (or "Lord of hosts") is used more than two hundred times in the Old Testament (see 1 Samuel 17:45 and Isaiah 9:6-7, among others). This simple title reveals quite a bit about the nature of God.

The word "hosts" here refers to the angels in heaven rather than the Eucharist. It emphasizes God's ultimate power over all of his creation and all of his creatures, both in heaven and on earth; it proclaims him to be almighty. "God of hosts," then, is a statement not only of God's ultimate power but also of our subjection to that power. No one stands before God except by his power,

mercy, and grace. We can only approach God because of his love for us, because of Christ's sacrifice for us (see Hebrews 4:16).

If you would like to read more instances where God is referred to as "God of hosts," check out a Bible concordance (a list of Scripture verses that contain a specific word or phrase) or the index at the back of your Bible for a list of every reference. Spend some time in the book of Psalms (especially Psalms 46 and 84) and in Isaiah, Jeremiah, Zechariah, and Malachi.

7. May We Merit

Those of you who attend Catholic schools might be familiar with the term "demerit." A demerit is something that is usually "earned" or given out when a behavior is not what it should be or is not up to acceptable standards. You may earn a demerit because you talk back to a teacher, fail to listen, or forget to do your homework. Demerits, then, are handed out based on behavior and are used as a tool.

To "merit" something, on the other hand, has an opposite, positive meaning. When we merit something, our actions bring us a reward. When we pray, "May we merit," it is with the understanding that *everything* God gives us is given freely. It is *grace*. As we have seen, grace is God's life in us. We do not deserve it, and we cannot earn it. God grants us his grace because he loves us and wants to share his life with us.

When we say, "May we merit," what we are really asking is, "Lord, may our words and actions demonstrate that we desire your goodness." Just as we get a demerit for doing something contrary to God's law, we should seek to live in a way that merits the kind of grace God wants to give us.

Remember—when we pray that our actions may merit God's blessings, we are not asking for our actions to *cause* God to give us grace. We do not control God by our actions; he gives us his grace freely, as a gift of his love. We cannot earn his love or salvation. (This is actually a heresy called "Pelagianism.") We are praying that our actions are worthy of the love God pours out on us, that we are living in a way that shows how thankful we are for the free gift of his love. When you hear the words, "May we merit," challenge yourself to change your actions and praise so that they are worthy of such a gift.

8. Abasement

A basement is the place in your parents' house where you will live if you don't study hard and get a job, right? *(Ha. Ha.)* Actually, "abasement" does have some relationship to the basement of a house. Both words are used to describe the low point, something at the "base," at the bottom or lower level. Abasement means being in a "lowered state" or a "lesser status," and is typically used to describe the state of Jesus in relationship to God the Father. We need to understand this correctly, though. It does not mean that Jesus is "lower" than God, since he himself is divine. It refers to the fact that Jesus humbled himself to be born "in the likeness of man" (see 1 Philippians 2:7).

When you hear the word "abasement" in the prayers of the Mass, think of the ways that you need to be humbled by God. Though Jesus did not have anything he needed to be "lifted out of" because he was perfect and without sin, you and I certainly do. We need to be lifted up by God from our own struggles, selfishness, and sins. Jesus humbly accepted to be born in our human likeness so that he could lift us up to him.

9. Partake

Picture your childhood playground. Two team captains begin choosing players for an intense game of kickball. There you stand, anxiously waiting to be picked, agonizing over when your name will be called.

Fast forward several years. At school, you hear people talking about an upcoming party but you have not received an invitation yet. You begin to feel excluded and a bit sad.

We all want to be invited. Nobody wants to be excluded, on the outside looking in. This is human nature. Even if you are a little shy or an introvert and the thought of interacting and socializing with people is scary, you would still like to be invited. Invitations make us feel affirmed and validated. They give us a sense of belonging and community.

This desire for community and to be in communion with one another is a gift from God. We are designed to be together. We are born into families and communities.

It is through relationships that we learn how to love, to receive love, and to grow in love.

The word "partake" literally means to "take part in" something or to join in an activity. In Mass, you will hear this term used in the Eucharistic Prayer.

Jesus is not picking you for kickball or inviting you to a party. He is sending you a personal invitation to his own wedding feast. As it says in Scripture, "Blessed are those who are invited to the marriage supper of the Lamb" (Revelation 19:9). Jesus, the Lamb, is the Groom, and the Church is his bride (see Revelation 19:7; Ephesians 5:23; and Matthew 22:2). The Mass is not just a sacrifice; it is also a wedding feast.

During Mass, we are invited to partake of the heavenly wedding between Christ and the Church. We are not there as guests for the food. Nor are we there to serve as bridesmaids or groomsmen. We are there to "get married," to unite ourselves to God and partake of his very life. We say "partake" rather than "share" because we are so intimately involved in this celebration.

Nothing on earth could be a greater validation of our worth and dignity than for the God of the universe to invite us into a personal and intimate relationship with him. So you are being invited to the greatest wedding in history. Do you accept this invitation to partake? Your life is your "RSVP."

10. Implore

My heart was slowly shattering into a million pieces. I was standing in the toy aisle at a store with the cutest little three-year-old face staring back at me. My youngest daughter was clutching a box with both hands, begging me—through tear-filled eyes—to buy her a new mermaid toy.

As a good father, not wanting to raise a spoiled child (and fully aware of the fact that we already have six thousand mermaids in our home), I gently said, "No, sweetie, you don't need another mermaid. I'm sorry."

It was at this point that the tears, a slowly leaking faucet up until now, shot forth like an exploding fire hydrant. "PPPLLLLEEEAAASSSSEEE Daddy!" she exclaimed through pouting lips.

Anyone watching witnessed two things. First, they witnessed a three-year-old master of manipulation. Back then, she could have negotiated the release of hostages during a bank robbery. Second, they observed the difference between "asking" and "imploring."

The word "implore" comes from a Latin term meaning "to invoke (beg for) with tears." Imploring is more than a civil request between two equals; it is an earnest request, filled with humility, made from someone who is "lower" than another. While my daughter and I have equal human dignity, I have authority over her as her father. In that sense, we are not equal. She depends on me for food, clothes, lodging, and, in this case, mermaid paraphernalia.

She was imploring me to hear her cry and "answer her prayer" for yet another doll. Her disposition was one of humility toward her father, begging through teary eyes for her heart's deepest request.

When we implore God during the Mass, we are doing much the same thing. We are acknowledging that while God is approachable, we are not on his level. We approach him in humility with earnestness and sincerity, begging him—sometimes even to the point of tears—to hear our prayers and respond according to his will.

Of course, my daughter did not really care about whether or not it was my will, she just wanted the mermaid ... but you get the idea.

By saying, "We implore you," or, "We beseech you," to God, we are publicly praising God while also acknowledging that we understand the difference—and even the "distance"—between God's divinity and our humanity.

During the *epiclesis* (when the priest lowers his hands over the gifts of bread and wine) he says:

> *Therefore, O Lord, we humbly **implore** you: by the same Spirit graciously make holy these gifts we have brought to you for consecration, that they may become the Body and Blood of your Son our Lord Jesus Christ ...*

Notice the posture of the prayer: We are imploring God, begging him for our heart's truest desire, which we find in the Eucharist. We are his children, coming before him with our hopes and fears and begging him not only to fulfill our needs but, once again, to exceed them. This is an act of humility on our part but not presumption. We should not expect God to be our "genie," granting our every wish, but rather to be our Father fulfilling our every need through his graciousness and mercy.

Oh, and by the way, my daughter got the mermaid. Fathers want more for their children than the children ever do. God the Father is no different. Go to him.

11. Chalice

Before the new translation of the Mass was instituted in 2011, we used the word "cup" quite a bit during the Liturgy. We would pray and sing things like "when we eat this bread and drink this *cup*." The difficulty with the word "cup" is that there are many different types of cups. We have coffee cups, paper cups, plastic cups, and glasses. Every now and then, when there is something to celebrate, we may use our most prized cup—the commemorative *Star Wars* cup from Pizza Hut, for example. This cup, though, is used only when there is something to celebrate, when we have a reason to use it. And we tend to be very careful with it. If it is on the table, we know something exciting is happening, and our energy automatically causes us to focus more during that meal.

The cup used during Mass, however, in which the priest consecrates and we receive the Precious Blood of Christ is referred to in the current translation of the Mass as the "chalice." The Latin word for this special cup is *calix*, and it has a different meaning than just "cup." During Mass, the word chalice is used because this cup is not ordinary. This reminds us that something unique is happening during Mass. Chalices should be made of "noble" material befitting the Eucharist.

They must be unbreakable and made of a precious metal, usually gold or silver.

A chalice was used in ancient Jewish rituals, such as the Passover, to show the importance of the meal that celebrated God's covenant with Israel. The priest Melchizedek made his offering in a chalice (see Genesis 14:18), and Jesus himself used a special cup (the Passover cup) at the Last Supper (see Matthew 26:27). Though modern English versions of the Bible may use the word "cup" in these instances, the official Latin translation of the Bible, the Vulgate, uses the word *calix*. The Church, in its wisdom, has chosen to use the word "chalice" to emphasize the unique nature of what is being celebrated at the Mass.

12. Thrones and Dominions

People seem to be fascinated by angels. In television, film, and songs, artists offer varying "interpretations" regarding angels, including what they look like and how they behave. Some people mistakenly think we become angels after we die. We do not. We can become saints but not angels.

The name "angel" comes from the Greek word *angelos* (Hebrew *malakh*), meaning "messenger." In both the Old and New Testaments, angels bring God's message to human beings. It was the archangel Gabriel who announced to Mary that God had chosen her to be mother of the Messiah (see Luke 1:26-38).

The existence of angels is a truth of our Faith that Christ himself attested to in the Gospels. Angels are pure spirits; they have no physical bodies. Angels do, however, occasionally take on "human form" or appearance (see Tobit). Angels are "constantly beholding the face of God" (see Matthew 18:10 and Psalm 103:20).

Christian tradition has maintained that every human being is given a guardian angel at birth.

In the fourth century, the Church Fathers began to write about the different "ranks" or "choirs" of angels. Each choir has specific missions and activities, though all share the same angelic nature. The traditional "ranks" of angels are the following:

- Seraphim
- Cherubim
- Thrones
- Dominions
- Virtues
- Powers
- Principalities
- Archangels
- Angels

Seraphim, cherubim, and thrones are dedicated to the contemplation of God, while dominions, virtues, and powers are given responsibility over the universe in its totality. Principalities, archangels, and angels are dedicated as God's messengers to humanity. St. Paul spoke about these powers and purposes in his letter to the Colossians (see 1:16).

In Mass, then, when you hear "thrones and dominions" mentioned in the Eucharistic Prayer, this refers to these specific "ranks" of angels to remind us of the angels' presence during the Mass. This invites us to think more deeply about the power, purpose, and role of angels in our daily lives. You can read more about angels in the *Catechism* (see CCC 327–336).

13. We Venerate

Think about the family room in your home. You probably feel quite comfortable in it. You can take your shoes off, put your feet up, let the snack crumbs fall where they may, right? (At least until Mom gets home.)

Now, imagine you are at the Vatican. You have been invited into the pope's private office. It is doubtful that you will rip open a bag of chips, kick off your shoes, and put your feet up on the Holy Father's desk.

Why not? Because how we interact with our surroundings—what actions are appropriate— has everything to do with where we are. Certain behaviors are appropriate in some places but not in others. Cheering and screaming is OK, even expected, at a sporting event but not in a church. Some places are worthy of more "restrained" behavior; they are worthy of reverence, of "veneration."

To "venerate" something or someone means to act in a way that outwardly demonstrates our great respect and awe. It is an acknowledgment that we understand that where we are or what we are doing is special.

What we are saying with our words and actions when we venerate God during Mass is that this event is beyond all other events. Even more fundamentally, we are saying that God is the source of everything in his creation, including our very lives.

While God alone is worthy of adoration and worship—the highest form of veneration—we also venerate holy people (saints), places (churches, shrines), and things (crucifixes, relics) because of their relationship with the all-holy God. Through our veneration of saints and holy places, we demonstrate our belief that they are different than the rest of the world (i.e., that they reflect the next world to which we have been called).

Venerating the saints and holy things is a great way to remind ourselves about what is most important in life. While there is nothing wrong with being passionate about sports, music, hobbies, or your friends, there should be a different part of your heart and soul reserved for those things God gives us to cheer us on to heaven.

Remember—Jesus told his disciples that, "Where your treasure is, there will your heart be also" (see Matthew 6:21). We venerate what we treasure most. Hopefully, God is number one in your heart, because you are number one in his.

14. Serene and Kindly Countenance

When we think of making a happy face, it can mean everything from a text message abbreviation with a colon and parenthesis to a smile before the camera flash. In a different way, we can sometimes just look at the face of someone we know well and immediately know that something is wrong—or that there is something to celebrate.

Our "countenance" is our facial expression. When we speak of the "countenance of the Lord," we are speaking of his face, though not literally. We mean his very presence and approval, his love and care for us. If you have been blessed enough to have a grandfather in your life, you might remember being a small child and crawling into his lap. Looking up at him, you could see in his face a radiance and a love for you that made you know that nothing else mattered in the world.

Similarly, when we speak of God the Father's countenance as "serene and kindly," we are talking about the characteristics of his love, echoing the words of Scripture: "The Lord make his face [countenance] shine upon you, and be gracious to you" (Numbers 6:25). When the priest asks the Lord to "be pleased to look upon these offerings with serene and kindly countenance," he is asking for the very face of God to look upon them and accept them with his loving and kindly gaze. By extension, we are asking God to look upon us lovingly because we are his, and his every desire is to show us his love.

At Mass, we encounter the love of God in the deepest way possible in this life, which prepares us for the day when we will experience God's radiance "face to face" in heaven.

15. Our Oblations

Sometimes, as we are about to run out the door on the way to a birthday party or to a Mother's Day brunch, we suddenly realize the gift we have bought does not really expresses our love for that person. Or maybe a sibling just hands us a card and we sign it, without even knowing what gift is attached to it. When the person thanks us, we tell them they are welcome, but we have not really offered them anything from our heart. We have just gone through the motions out of a sense of obligation or habit, because it seemed like the right thing to do.

At Mass, we are invited to a sacrifice, where we are asked to do more than just casually bring any old gift. While we do participate in offering the gifts of bread and wine, our financial support, and our prayer, we are called to offer our "oblations" on the altar to God. Let's see what this means.

The word "oblation" is from a Latin root meaning "offering." You will hear the priest use this word in the First and Third Eucharistic Prayers. As you hear the priest make that offering, call yourself to do more than just "sign your name on the card." Give a pure, true offering by placing your own life on the altar along with the gifts of bread and wine.

The oblation we offer to God includes our very lives, our willingness to obey him in all things, and our desire to participate fully in the Sacrifice of the Mass.

16. Your Elect

All of us have been in situations where we wanted to be included, to be a part of the "group." Whether it is a group that we have not quite been a part of, a team we wanted to play on, or a party we were not invited to, we want to be a part of the action. Even having someone hold out on accepting our friendship online can feel like rejection while we wait in a state of "purgatory" to be told "yes."

Do we need to worry about being accepted by God? It seems strange to think that there are some God likes—his "elect"—and some he does not. Even if we are pretty confident that we are on the "in list," this does not sound like a God who desires that all might be saved (see 1 Timothy 2:4). But when we hear in the Third Eucharistic Prayer the hope that "we may obtain an inheritance with your elect," we are not saying that God loves some more than others. Rather, we are acknowledging that there are some who have reached eternal unity with God—that is, they are in heaven already. The elect of whom we speak in this moment are God's *chosen ones*, and the prayer specifically includes the Blessed Virgin Mary and the saints.

So the phrase "your elect" refers to those who have been "set apart" to be in union with Jesus forever in heaven. This does not imply that the elect have been predetermined by God; they have desired to live holy lives and be with him for eternity. God freely gives us his grace, so we have the power to do his will and avoid sin. As we participate in the Mass, we should pray also that we live lives worthy of becoming saints. If there has ever been a group we should want to be a part of, this is the one. To be one of God's elect is his greatest desire for you, so make it your desire as well.

17. *Kyrie Eleison, Agnus Dei, Miserere Nobis*

How many languages do you speak? One? Two? You might be surprised, actually ...

It hit me recently how many people probably do not know the exact meaning of the "foreign" liturgical phrases we pray at Mass. What hit me even harder was how often I say or sing a response at Mass out of habit, without really pausing and praying the words I am singing or saying.

Here are some of the foreign phrases you hear at Mass: *Kyrie eleison, Agnus Dei,* and *Miserere nobis.*

What do they *mean*, though?

Kyrie eleison – Greek for "Lord, have mercy."
Christe eleison – Greek for "Christ, have mercy."
Agnus Dei – Latin for "Lamb of God."
Miserere nobis – Latin for "Have mercy on us."
Qui tollis peccata mundi – Latin for "Who takes away the sins of the world."
Dona nobis pacem – Latin for "Grant us peace."

Even if you already know the meanings of these phrases, you should ask yourself, "Am I simply repeating these phrases, or am I really praying them with my whole heart when I say or sing them?"

Consider these words from the psalm: "My lips will shout for joy as I sing your praise; my soul, too, which you have redeemed" (Psalm 71:23, NAB).

This verse is a reminder to us that our worship is intended to be a spirit-filled response to the greatness and love of God. When we sing or respond during Mass, it should never be an habitual, half-hearted, and half-audible reply but rather a joyful shout from the depths of our souls (though "shout" here does not imply "loud"!). This verse also tells us that singing invites, involves, and ignites our souls; at Mass, singing is not merely a physical act but also a spiritual one.

When singing these phrases, we are not merely reciting some "dead" language; we are communicating spiritually, asking the Lamb of God (Jesus) to have mercy on us for our sins. We are asking him to give us his grace and peace of mind, heart, and soul.

These languages are not dead because they continue to be prayed at Mass throughout the world.

Holy Days of Obligation

We might also call these "holy days of *opportunity*"—the opportunity to grow in holiness, that is. In the United States, the following six solemnities are holy days of obligation on which we are required to attend Mass:

- January 1 – **Mary, Mother of God**
- Thursday, sixth week of Easter – **Ascension**
- August 15 – **Assumption** of the Blessed Virgin Mary
- November 1 – **All Saints**
- December 8 – **Immaculate Conception**
- December 25 – **Christmas**

In most dioceses in the United States, the solemnity of the Ascension is actually celebrated on the following Sunday. Easter, the most important solemnity of the Church's liturgical year, does not appear on the list because it is always on a Sunday. Note that when January 1, August 15, or November 1 occurs on a Saturday or on a Monday, they are *not* holy days of obligation in the United States.

Liturgical Seasons

Just as there are four "earthly" seasons of spring, summer, fall, and winter, the Church divides its liturgical year (which begins on the first Sunday in Advent) into seasons.

The Church has "scheduled" the liturgical seasons to follow the chronological flow of important feasts and solemnities. Each liturgical season has a specific color, special prayers, and dedicated hymns and music to help draw us into deeper spiritual contemplation.

The following are the seasons of the Church's liturgical year.

Advent

The Advent season begins the Church year. It starts on the fourth Sunday before Christmas and lasts four weeks—as indicated by the four candles on the Advent wreath found in every parish church.

Liturgical colors: violet. Symbolizes penance and humility as we prepare our hearts to celebrate the coming of Jesus at Christmas. On the third Sunday of Advent (traditionally known as *Gaudete* Sunday, from the Latin word "rejoice," indicating that Christ's birth is near), the priest may wear rose-colored vestments.

Christmas

The Christmas season begins with the Solemnity of the Nativity (Christmas) and continues until the feast of the Baptism of Our Lord, which occurs on the Sunday following January 6.

Liturgical color: white (or gold). Represents light, purity, joy, and glory.

Ordinary Time

Despite its name, this liturgical season is not "ordinary" as in "less important." It really is "ordered." Ordinary Time "bridges" the other liturgical seasons and keeps the spiritual rhythm of the liturgical year by walking us through the Gospels, unpacking the Christian life.

Ordinary Time has two parts. The first part begins on the Monday following the Baptism of Our Lord and lasts until Ash Wednesday, and the second part begins on Pentecost Monday and lasts to the First Sunday of Advent. This makes it the longest season of the Church's liturgical year.

Liturgical color: green. Symbolizes hope, eternal life, and growth.

Lent

Lent begins on Ash Wednesday and helps us to repent and live the gospel more closely during the following forty days. (Note that the Sundays of Lent are not technically considered part of the Lenten season and are not counted among the forty days.)

Lent lasts until the *Triduum*, which begins on Holy Thursday and includes Good Friday and Holy Saturday.

Liturgical color: violet. Represents penance and humility, reminding us to seek reconciliation.

Easter

We usually think of Easter as a day, but our celebration of the Lord's resurrection actually lasts for fifty days and goes up to Pentecost Sunday. ("Pentecost" means the "fiftieth day.")

Liturgical colors: white. Symbolizes light, purity, and joy in celebration of the resurrection of Christ.

The other liturgical color you will see used on special feasts and occasions in this season is red. On Pentecost, red is worn to remind us of the fire of the Holy Spirit that descended upon the apostles; on the feast days of martyrs, red is used to symbolize the blood they shed in witness to the gospel of Christ.

Introduction to the Cycle of Sunday Scripture Readings

The Church is very wise. It gives us an incredible gift in the readings of the Sacred Scriptures we hear proclaimed at every Mass. The Scripture readings are placed into two "cycles," a weekday cycle and a Sunday cycle. This method ensures that we receive the fullness of God's Word in a systematic and intentional way.

You will notice that there are three Scripture readings and a Responsorial Psalm at every Sunday Mass—making a total of four readings from the Bible. They have been chosen and grouped together for a specific reason. When you read and pray through them, you will notice a "strand" or "theme" that ties them all together. This theme usually forms the focus of the priest's homily.

The Sunday cycle is divided into three "years" of readings and are labeled "A, B, and C," each of which focuses on a different Gospel. Year A focuses on Matthew, Year B on Mark (as well as John, Chapter 6), and Year C on Luke. During the Easter season, we hear mainly from the Gospel of John. The Sunday cycles change on the First Sunday of Advent because Advent is the beginning of the liturgical year.

On the following pages, you will find the three cycles of Sunday readings. (Note that the Responsorial Psalm is not included.) Take some time to read them ahead of time, and you will be amazed at how your experience during the Liturgy of the Word will come to life in a new way. If you are wondering what Sunday is next, check your parish bulletin (usually on the front or the first page) or parish website.

Getting more out of Mass is as easy as reading ahead. It is as simple as A, B, C …

CYCLE A

(Used in 2017, 2020, 2023, 2026)

Advent Season

1st Sunday of Advent
1) Isaiah 2:1-5
2) Romans 13:11-14
3) Matthew 24:37-44

2nd Sunday of Advent
1) Isaiah 11:1-10
2) Romans 15:4-9
3) Matthew 3:1-12

3rd Sunday of Advent
1) Isaiah 35:1-6a, 10
2) James 5:7-10
3) Matthew 11:2-11

4th Sunday of Advent
1) Isaiah 7:10-14
2) Romans 1:1-7
3) Matthew 1:18-24

Christmas Season

Christmas Vigil
1) Isaiah 62:1-5
2) Acts 13:16-17, 22-25
3) Matthew 1:1-25

Christmas (Mass at midnight)
1) Isaiah 9:1-6
2) Titus 2:11-14
3) Luke 2:1-14

Christmas (Mass at dawn)
1) Isaiah 62:11-12
2) Titus 3:4-7
3) Luke 2:15-20

**Christmas
(Mass during the day)**
1) Isaiah 52:7-10
2) Hebrews 1:1-6

3) John 1:1-18

**Sunday after Christmas
(Holy Family)**
1) Sirach 3:2-6, 12-14
2) Colossians 3:12-21
3) Matthew 2:13-15, 19-23

January 1 (Solemnity of Mary, Mother of God)
1) Numbers 6:22-27
2) Galatians 4:4-7
3) Luke 2:16-21

2nd Sunday after Christmas
1) Sirach 24:1-2, 8-12
2) Ephesians 1:3-6, 15-18
3) John 1:1-18

Epiphany
1) Isaiah 60:1-6
2) Ephesians 3:2-3a, 5-6
3) Matthew 2:1-12

**Sunday after Epiphany
(Baptism of the Lord)**
1) Isaiah 42:1-4, 6-7
2) Acts 10:34-38
3) Matthew 3:13-17

Lenten Season

Ash Wednesday
1) Joel 2:12-18
2) 2 Corinthians 5:20–6:2
3) Matthew 6:1-6, 16-18

1st Sunday of Lent
1) Genesis 2:7-9, 3:1-7
2) Romans 5:12-19
3) Matthew 4:1-11

2nd Sunday of Lent
1) Genesis 12:1-4a
2) 2 Timothy 1:8b-10
3) Matthew 17:1-9

3rd Sunday of Lent
1) Exodus 17:3-7
2) Romans 5:1-2, 5-8
3) John 4:5-42

4th Sunday of Lent
1) 1 Samuel 16:1b, 6-7, 10-13a
2) Ephesians 5:8-14
3) John 9:1-41

5th Sunday of Lent
1) Ezekiel 37:12-14
2) Romans 8:8-11
3) John 11:1-45

**Passion Sunday
(Palm Sunday)**
Procession: Matthew 21:1-11
1) Isaiah 50:4-7
2) Philippians 2:6-11
3) Matthew 26:14–27:66

Easter Triduum and Easter Season

**Mass of Lord's Supper
(Holy Thursday)**
1) Exodus 12:1-8, 11-14
2) 1 Corinthians 11:23-26
3) John 13:1-15

Good Friday
1) Isaiah 52:13–53:12
2) Hebrews 4:14-16, 5:7-9
3) John 18:1–19:42

Easter Vigil
1) Genesis 1:1–2:2
   Genesis 22:1-18
   Exodus 14:15–15:1
   Isaiah 54:5-14
   Isaiah 55:1-11
   Baruch 3:9-15, 32–4:4
   Ezekiel 36:16-28

2) Romans 6:3-11

3) Matthew 28:1-10

Easter Sunday

1) Acts 10:34a, 37-43

2) Colossians 3:1-4
   or 1 Corinthians 5:6b-8

3) John 20:1-9
   or Matthew 28:1-10
   Evening: Luke 24:13-35

2nd Sunday of Easter

1) Acts 2:42-47

2) 1 Peter 1:3-9

3) John 20:19-31

3rd Sunday of Easter

1) Acts 2:14, 22-28

2) 1 Peter 1:17-21

3) Luke 24:13-35

4th Sunday of Easter

1) Acts 2:14a, 36-41

2) 1 Peter 2:20b-25

3) John 10:1-10

5th Sunday of Easter

1) Acts 6:1-7

2) 1 Peter 2:4-9

3) John 14:1-12

6th Sunday of Easter

1) Acts 8:5-8, 14-17

2) 1 Peter 3:15-18

3) John 14:15-21

Ascension of Our Lord

1) Acts 1:1-11

2) Ephesians 1:17-23

3) Matthew 28:16-20

7th Sunday of Easter

1) Acts 1:12-14

2) 1 Peter 4:13-16

3) John 17:1-11a

Pentecost Vigil

1) Genesis 11:1-9
   Exodus 19:3-8a, 16-20b
   Ezekiel 37:1-14
   Joel 3:1-5

2) Romans 8:22-27

3) John 7:37-39

Pentecost
(Mass during the day)

1) Acts 2:1-11

2) 1 Corinthians 12:3b-7, 12-13

3) John 20:19-23

Solemnities of the Lord during Ordinary Time

Trinity Sunday
(Sunday after Pentecost)

1) Exodus 34:4b-6, 8-9

2) 2 Corinthians 13:11-13

3) John 3:16-18

Corpus Christi

1) Deuteronomy 8:2-3, 14b-16a

2) 1 Corinthians 10:16-17

3) John 6:51-58

Sacred Heart of Jesus

1) Deuteronomy 7:6-11

2) 1 John 4:7-16

3) Matthew 11:25-30

Ordinary Time

1st Sunday
(See Baptism of the Lord)

2nd Sunday

1) Isaiah 49:3, 5-6

2) 1 Corinthians 1:1-3

3) John 1:29-34

3rd Sunday

1) Isaiah 8:23b–9:3

2) 1 Corinthians 1:10-13, 17

3) Matthew 4:12-23

4th Sunday

1) Zephaniah 2:3, 3:12-13

2) 1 Corinthians 1:26-31

3) Matthew 5:1-12a

5th Sunday

1) Isaiah 58:7-10

2) 1 Corinthians 2:1-5

3) Matthew 5:13-16

6th Sunday

1) Sirach 15:15-20

2) 1 Corinthians 2:6-10

3) Matthew 5:17-37

7th Sunday

1) Leviticus 19:1-2, 17-18

2) 1 Corinthians 3:16-23

3) Matthew 5:38-48

8th Sunday

1) Isaiah 49:14-15

2) 1 Corinthians 4:1-5

3) Matthew 6:24-34

9th Sunday

1) Deuteronomy 11:18, 26-28

2) Romans 3:21-25a, 28

3) Matthew 7:21-27

10th Sunday

1) Hosea 6:3-6

2) Romans 4:18-25

3) Matthew 9:9-13

11th Sunday

1) Exodus 19:2-6a

2) Romans 5:6-11

3) Matthew 9:36–10:8

12th Sunday

1) Jeremiah 20:10-13

2) Romans 5:12-15

3) Matthew 10:26-33

13th Sunday

1) 2 Kings 4:8-11, 14-16a

2) Romans 6:3-4, 8-11
3) Matthew 10:37-42

14th Sunday
1) Zechariah 9:9-10
2) Romans 8:9, 11-13
3) Matthew 11:25-30

15th Sunday
1) Isaiah 55:10-11
2) Romans 8:18-23
3) Matthew 13:1-23

16th Sunday
1) Wisdom 12:13, 16-19
2) Romans 8:26-27
3) Matthew 13:24-43

17th Sunday
1) 1 Kings 3:5, 7-12
2) Romans 8:28-30
3) Matthew 13:44-52

18th Sunday
1) Isaiah 55:1-3
2) Romans 8:35, 37-39
3) Matthew 14:13-21

19th Sunday
1) 1 Kings 19:9a, 11-13a
2) Romans 9:1-5
3) Matthew 14:22-33

20th Sunday
1) Isaiah 56:1, 6-7
2) Romans 11:13-15, 29-32

3) Matthew 15:21-28

21st Sunday
1) Isaiah 22:19-23
2) Romans 11:33-36
3) Matthew 16:13-20

22nd Sunday
1) Jeremiah 20:7-9
2) Romans 12:1-2
3) Matthew 16:21-27

23rd Sunday
1) Ezekiel 33:7-9
2) Romans 13:8-10
3) Matthew 18:15-20

24th Sunday
1) Sirach 27:30–28:7
2) Romans 14:7-9
3) Matthew 18:21-35

25th Sunday
1) Isaiah 55:6-9
2) Philippians 1:20c-24, 27a
3) Matthew 20:1-16a

26th Sunday
1) Ezekiel 18:25-28
2) Philippians 2:1-11
3) Matthew 21:28-32

27th Sunday
1) Isaiah 5:1-7
2) Philippians 4:6-9
3) Matthew 21:33-43

28th Sunday
1) Isaiah 25:6-10a
2) Philippians 4:12-14, 19-20
3) Matthew 22:1-14

29th Sunday
1) Isaiah 45:1, 4-6
2) 1 Thessalonians 1:1-5b
3) Matthew 22:15-21

30th Sunday
1) Exodus 22:20-26
2) 1 Thessalonians 1:5c-10
3) Matthew 22:34-40

31st Sunday
1) Malachi 1:14b–2:2b, 8-10
2) 1 Thessalonians 2:7b-9, 13
3) Matthew 23:1-12

32nd Sunday
1) Wisdom 6:12-16
2) 1 Thessalonians 4:13-18
3) Matthew 25:1-13

33rd Sunday
1) Proverbs 31:10-13, 19-20, 30-31
2) 1 Thessalonians 5:1-6
3) Matthew 25:14-30

34th Sunday (Christ the King)
1) Ezekiel 34:11-12, 15-17
2) 1 Corinthians 15:20-26, 28
3) Matthew 25:31-46

CYCLE B

(Used in 2015, 2018, 2021, 2024)

Advent Season

1st Sunday of Advent
1) Isaiah 63:16b-17, 19b, 64:2-7
2) 1 Corinthians 1:3-9

3) Mark 13:33-37

2nd Sunday of Advent
1) Isaiah 40:1-5, 9-11
2) 2 Peter 3:8-14
3) Mark 1:1-8

3rd Sunday of Advent
1) Isaiah 61:1-2a, 10-11

2) 1 Thessalonians 5:16-24
3) John 1:6-8, 19-28

4th Sunday of Advent
1) 2 Samuel 7:1-5, 8-12, 14a, 16
2) Romans 16:25-27
3) Luke 1:26-38

Christmas Season

Christmas Vigil
1) Isaiah 62:1-5
2) Acts 13:16-17, 22-25
3) Matthew 1:1-25

Christmas (Mass at midnight)
1) Isaiah 9:1-6
2) Titus 2:11-14
3) Luke 2:1-14

Christmas (Mass at dawn)
1) Isaiah 62:11-12
2) Titus 3:4-7
3) Luke 2:15-20

Christmas (Mass during the day)
1) Isaiah 52:7-10
2) Hebrews 1:1-6
3) John 1:1-18

Sunday after Christmas (Holy Family)
1) Genesis 15:1-6; 21:1-3
2) Hebrews 11:8, 11-12, 17-19
3) Luke 2:22-40

January 1 (Solemnity of Mary, Mother of God)
1) Numbers 6:22-27
2) Galatians 4:4-7
3) Luke 2:16-21

2nd Sunday after Christmas
1) Sirach 24:1-2, 8-12
2) Ephesians 1:3-6, 15-18
3) John 1:1-18

Epiphany
1) Isaiah 60:1-6
2) Ephesians 3:2-3a, 5-6
3) Matthew 2:1-12

Sunday after Epiphany (Baptism of the Lord)
1) Isaiah 42:1-4, 6-7
2) Acts 10:34-38
3) Mark 1:6b-11

Lenten Season

Ash Wednesday
1) Joel 2:12-18
2) 2 Corinthians 5:20–6:2
3) Matthew 6:1-6, 16-18

1st Sunday of Lent
1) Genesis 9:8-15
2) 1 Peter 3:18-22
3) Mark 1:12-15

2nd Sunday of Lent
1) Genesis 22:1-2, 9a, 10-13, 15-18
2) Romans 8:31b-34
3) Mark 9:2-10

3rd Sunday of Lent
1) Exodus 20:1-17
2) 1 Corinthians 1:22-25
3) John 2:13-25

4th Sunday of Lent
1) 2 Chronicles 36:14-16, 19-23
2) Ephesians 2:4-10
3) John 3:14-21

5th Sunday of Lent
1) Jeremiah 31:31-34
2) Hebrews 5:7-9
3) John 12:20-33

Passion Sunday (Palm Sunday)
Procession: Mark 11:1-10 or John 12:12-16
1) Isaiah 50:4-7
2) Philippians 2:6-11
3) Mark 14:1–15:47

Easter Triduum and Easter Season

Mass of Lord's Supper (Holy Thursday)
1) Exodus 12:1-8, 11-14
2) 1 Corinthians 11:23-26
3) John 13:1-15

Good Friday
1) Isaiah 52:13–53:12
2) Hebrews 4:14-16, 5:7-9
3) John 18:1–19:42

Easter Vigil
1) Genesis 1:1–2:2
   Genesis 22:1-18
   Exodus 14:15–15:1
   Isaiah 54:5-14
   Isaiah 55:1-11
   Baruch 3:9-15, 32–4:4
   Ezekiel 36:16-28
2) Romans 6:3-11
3) Mark 16:1-8

Easter Sunday
1) Acts 10:34a, 37-43
2) Colossians 3:1-4 or 1 Corinthians 5:6b-8
3) John 20:1-9 or Mark 16:1-8
   Evening: Luke 24:13-35

2nd Sunday of Easter
1) Acts 4:32-35
2) 1 John 5:1-6
3) John 20:19-31

3rd Sunday of Easter
1) Acts 3:13-15, 17-19
2) 1 John 2:1-5a
3) Luke 24:35-48

4th Sunday of Easter
1) Acts 4:8-12
2) 1 John 3:1-2

3) John 10:11-18

5th Sunday of Easter
1) Acts 9:26-31
2) 1 John 3:18-24
3) John 15:1-8

6th Sunday of Easter
1) Acts 10:25-26, 34-35, 44-48
2) 1 John 4:7-10
3) John 15:9-17

Ascension of Our Lord
1) Acts 1:1-11
2) Ephesians 1:17-23 or 4:1-13
3) Mark 16:15-20

7th Sunday of Easter
1) Acts 1:15-17, 20a, 20c-26
2) 1 John 4:11-16
3) John 17:11b-19

Pentecost Vigil
1) Genesis 11:1-9
   or Exodus 19:3-8a, 16-20b
   or Ezekiel 37:1-14
   or Joel 3:1-5
2) Romans 8:22-27
3) John 7:37-39

Pentecost
(Mass during the day)
1) Acts 2:1-11
2) 1 Corinthians 12:3b-7, 12-13
   or Galatians 5:16-25
3) John 20:19-23
   or John 15:26-27,16:12-15

Solemnities of the Lord during Ordinary Time

Trinity Sunday (Sunday after Pentecost)
1) Deuteronomy 4:32-34, 39-40
2) Romans 8:14-17

3) Matthew 28:16-20

Corpus Christi
1) Exodus 24:3-8
2) Hebrews 9:11-15
3) Mark 14:12-16, 22-26

Sacred Heart of Jesus
1) Hosea 11:1, 3-4, 8c-9
2) Ephesians 3:8-12, 14-19
3) John 19:31-37

Ordinary Time

1st Sunday
(See Baptism of the Lord)

2nd Sunday
1) 1 Samuel 3:3b-10, 19
2) 1 Corinthians 6:13c-15a, 17-20
3) John 1:35-42

3rd Sunday
1) Jonah 3:1-5, 10
2) 1 Corinthians 7:29-31
3) Mark 1:14-20

4th Sunday
1) Deuteronomy 18:15-20
2) 1 Corinthians 7:32-35
3) Mark 1:21-28

5th Sunday
1) Job 7:1-4, 6-7
2) 1 Corinthians 9:16-19, 22-23
3) Mark 1:29-39

6th Sunday
1) Leviticus 13:1-2, 44-46
2) 1 Corinthians 10:31–11:1
3) Mark 1:40-45

7th Sunday
1) Isaiah 43:18-19, 21-22, 24b-25
2) 2 Corinthians 1:18-22

3) Mark 2:1-12

8th Sunday
1) Hosea 2:16b, 17b, 21-22
2) 2 Corinthians 3:1b-6
3) Mark 2:18-22

9th Sunday
1) Deuteronomy 5:12-15
2) 2 Corinthians 4:6-11
3) Mark 2:23–3:6

10th Sunday
1) Genesis 3:9-15
2) 2 Corinthians 4:13–5:1
3) Mark 3:20-35

11th Sunday
1) Ezekiel 17:22-24
2) 2 Corinthians 5:6-10
3) Mark 4:26-34

12th Sunday
1) Job 38:1, 8-11
2) 2 Corinthians 5:14-17
3) Mark 4:35-41

13th Sunday
1) Wisdom 1:13-15, 2:23-24
2) 2 Corinthians 8:7, 9, 13-15
3) Mark 5:21-43

14th Sunday
1) Ezekiel 2:2-5
2) 2 Corinthians 12:7-10
3) Mark 6:1-6

15th Sunday
1) Amos 7:12-15
2) Ephesians 1:3-14
3) Mark 6:7-13

16th Sunday
1) Jeremiah 23:1-6
2) Ephesians 2:13-18
3) Mark 6:30-34

17th Sunday
1) 2 Kings 4:42-44
2) Ephesians 4:1-6
3) John 6:1-15

18th Sunday
1) Exodus 16:2-4, 12-15
2) Ephesians 4:17, 20-24
3) John 6:24-35

19th Sunday
1) 1 Kings 19:4-8
2) Ephesians 4:30—5:2
3) John 6:41-51

20th Sunday
1) Proverbs 9:1-6
2) Ephesians 5:15-20
3) John 6:51-58

21st Sunday
1) Joshua 24:1-2a, 15-17, 18b
2) Ephesians 5:21-32
3) John 6:60-69

22nd Sunday
1) Deuteronomy 4:1-2, 6-8
2) James 1:17-18, 21b-22, 27
3) Mark 7:1-8, 14-15, 21-23

23rd Sunday
1) Isaiah 35:4-7a
2) James 2:1-5
3) Mark 7:31-37

24th Sunday
1) Isaiah 50:5-9a
2) James 2:14-18
3) Mark 8:27-35

25th Sunday
1) Wisdom 2:12, 17-20
2) James 3:16—4:3
3) Mark 9:30-37

26th Sunday
1) Numbers 11:25-29
2) James 5:1-6
3) Mark 9:38-43, 45, 47-48

27th Sunday
1) Genesis 2:18-24
2) Hebrews 2:9-11
3) Mark 10:2-16

28th Sunday
1) Wisdom 7:7-11
2) Hebrews 4:12-13
3) Mark 10:17-30

29th Sunday
1) Isaiah 53:10-11
2) Hebrews 4:14-16
3) Mark 10:35-45

30th Sunday
1) Jeremiah 31:7-9
2) Hebrews 5:1-6
3) Mark 10:46-53

31st Sunday
1) Deuteronomy 6:2-6
2) Hebrews 7:23-28
3) Mark 12:28b-34

32nd Sunday
1) 1 Kings 17:10-16
2) Hebrews 9:24-28
3) Mark 12:38-44

33rd Sunday
1) Daniel 12:1-3
2) Hebrews 10:11-14, 18
3) Mark 13:24-32

34th Sunday (Christ the King)
1) Daniel 7:13-14
2) Revelation 1:5-8
3) John 18:33b-37

CYCLE C

(Used in 2016, 2019, 2022, 2025)

Advent Season

1st Sunday of Advent
1) Jeremiah 33:14-16
2) 1 Thessalonians 3:12—4:2
3) Luke 21:25-28, 34-36

2nd Sunday of Advent
1) Baruch 5:1-9
2) Philippians 1:4-6, 8-11
3) Luke 3:1-6

3rd Sunday of Advent
1) Zephaniah 3:14-18a
2) Philippians 4:4-7
3) Luke 3:10-18

4th Sunday of Advent
1) Micah 5:1-4a
2) Hebrews 10:5-10
3) Luke 1:39-45

Christmas Season

Christmas Vigil
1) Isaiah 62:1-6
2) Acts 13:16-17, 22-25
3) Matthew 1:1-25

Christmas (Mass at midnight)
1) Isaiah 9:1-6
2) Titus 2:11-14
3) Luke 2:1-14

Christmas (Mass at dawn)
1) Isaiah 62:11-12
2) Titus 3:4-7
3) Luke 2:15-20

Christmas (Mass during the day)
1) Isaiah 57:7-10

2) Hebrews 1:1-6

3) John 1:1-18

Sunday after Christmas (Holy Family)

1) 1 Samuel 1:19b-22, 24-28

2) 1 John 3:1-2, 21-24

3) Luke 2:41-52

January 1 (Solemnity of Mary, Mother of God)

1) Numbers 6:22-27

2) Galatians 4:4-7

3) Luke 2:16-21

2nd Sunday after Christmas

1) Sirach 24:1-2, 8-12

2) Ephesians 1:3-6, 15-18

3) John 1:1-18

Epiphany

1) Isaiah 60:1-6

2) Ephesians 3:2-3a, 5-6

3) Matthew 2:1-12

Sunday after Epiphany (Baptism of the Lord)

1) Isaiah 42:1-4, 6-7

2) Acts 10:34-38

3) Luke 3:15-16, 21-22

Lenten Season

Ash Wednesday

1) Joel 2:12-18

2) 2 Corinthians 5:20–6:2

3) Matthew 6:1-6, 16-18

1st Sunday of Lent

1) Deuteronomy 26:4-10

2) Romans 10:8-13

3) Luke 4:1-13

2nd Sunday of Lent

1) Genesis 15:5-12, 17-18

2) Philippians 3:17–4:1

3) Luke 9:28b-36

3rd Sunday of Lent

1) Exodus 3:1-8a, 13-15

2) 1 Corinthians 10:1-6, 10-12

3) Luke 13:1-9

4th Sunday of Lent

1) Joshua 5:9a, 10-12

2) 2 Corinthians 5:17-21

3) Luke 15:1-3, 11-32

5th Sunday of Lent

1) Isaiah 43:16-21

2) Philippians 3:8-14

3) John 8:1-11

Passion Sunday (Palm Sunday)

Procession: Luke 19:28-40

1) Isaiah 50:4-7

2) Philippians 2:6-11

3) Luke 22:14–23:56

Easter Triduum and Easter Season

Mass of Lord's Supper (Holy Thursday)

1) Exodus 12:1-8, 11-14

2) 1 Corinthians 11:23-26

3) John 13:1-15

Good Friday

1) Isaiah 52:13–53:12

2) Hebrews 4:14-16, 5:7-9

3) John 18:1–19:42

Easter Vigil

1) Genesis 1:1–2:2

   Genesis 22:1-18

   Exodus 14:15–15:1

   Isaiah 54:5-14

   Isaiah 55:1-11

   Baruch 3:9-15, 32–4:4

   Ezekiel 36:16-28

2) Romans 6:3-11

3) Luke 24:1-12

Easter Sunday

1) Acts 10:34a, 37-43

2) Colossians 3:1-4
   or 1 Corinthians 5:6b-8

3) John 20:1-9
   or Luke 24:1-12
   Evening: Luke 24:13-35

2nd Sunday of Easter

1) Acts 5:12-16

2) Revelation 1:9-11a, 12-13, 17-19

3) John 20:19-31

3rd Sunday of Easter

1) Acts 5:27b-32, 40b-41

2) Revelation 5:11-14

3) John 21:1-19

4th Sunday of Easter

1) Acts 13:14, 43-52

2) Revelation 7:9, 14b-17

3) John 10:27-30

5th Sunday of Easter

1) Acts 14:21-27

2) Revelation 21:1-5a

3) John 13:31-33a, 34-35

6th Sunday of Easter

1) Acts 15:1-2, 22-29

2) Revelation 21:10-14, 22-23

3) John 14:23-29

Ascension of the Lord

1) Acts 1:1-11

2) Ephesians 1:17-23
   or Hebrews 9:24-28, 10:19-23

3) Luke 24:46-53

7th Sunday of Easter

1) Acts 7:55-60

2) Revelation 22:12-14, 16-17, 20

3) John 17:20-26

Pentecost Vigil
1) Genesis 11:1-9
   or Exodus 19:3-8a, 16-20b
   or Ezekiel 37:1-14
   or Joel 3:1-5
2) Romans 8:22-27
3) John 7:37-39

Pentecost
(Mass during the day)
1) Acts 2:1-11
2) 1 Corinthians 12:3b-7, 12-13
   or Romans 8:8-27
3) John 20:19-23
   or John 14:15-16, 23b-26

Solemnities of the Lord during Ordinary

Trinity Sunday (Sunday after Pentecost)
1) Proverbs 8:22-31
2) Romans 5:1-5
3) John 16:12-15

Corpus Christi
1) Genesis 14:18-20
2) 1 Corinthians 11:23-26
3) Luke 9:11b-17

Sacred Heart of Jesus
1) Ezekiel 34:11-16
2) Romans 5:5-11
3) Luke 15:3-7

Ordinary Time

1st Sunday (See Baptism of the Lord)

2nd Sunday
1) Isaiah 62:1-5
2) 1 Corinthians 12:4-11
3) John 2:1-12

3rd Sunday
1) Nehemiah 8:1-4a, 5-6, 8-10
2) 1 Corinthians 12:12-30
3) Luke 1:1-4, 4:14-21

4th Sunday
1) Jeremiah 1:4-5, 17-19
2) 1 Corinthians 12:31–13:13
3) Luke 4:21-30

5th Sunday
1) Isaiah 6:1-2a, 3-8
2) 1 Corinthians 15:1-11
3) Luke 5:1-11

6th Sunday
1) Jeremiah 17:5-8
2) 1 Corinthians 15:12, 16-20
3) Luke 6:17, 20-26

7th Sunday
1) 1 Samuel 26:2, 7-9, 12-13, 22-23
2) 1 Corinthians 15:45-49
3) Luke 6:27-38

8th Sunday
1) Sirach 27:4-7
2) 1 Corinthians 15:54-58
3) Luke 6:39-45

9th Sunday
1) 1 Kings 8:41-43
2) Galatians 1:1-2, 6-10
3) Luke 7:1-10

10th Sunday
1) 1 Kings 17:17-24
2) Galatians 1:11-19
3) Luke 7:11-17

11th Sunday
1) 2 Samuel 12:7-10, 13
2) Galatians 2:16, 19-21
3) Luke 7:36–8:3

12th Sunday
1) Zechariah 12:10-11
2) Galatians 3:26-29
3) Luke 9:18-24

13th Sunday
1) 1 Kings 19:16b, 19-21
2) Galatians 5:1, 13-18
3) Luke 9:51-62

14th Sunday
1) Isaiah 66:10-14c
2) Galatians 6:14-18
3) Luke 10:1-12, 17-20

15th Sunday
1) Deuteronomy 30:10-14
2) Colossians 1:15-20
3) Luke 10:25-37

16th Sunday
1) Genesis 18:1-10a
2) Colossians 1:24-28
3) Luke 10:38-42

17th Sunday
1) Genesis 18:20-32
2) Colossians 2:12-14
3) Luke 11:1-13

18th Sunday
1) Ecclesiastes 1:2, 2:21-23
2) Colossians 3:1-5, 9-11
3) Luke 12:13-31

19th Sunday
1) Wisdom 18:6-9
2) Hebrews 11:1-2, 8-19
3) Luke 12:32-48

20th Sunday
1) Jeremiah 38:4-6, 8-10
2) Hebrews 12:1-4
3) Luke 12:49-53

21st Sunday
1) Isaiah 66:18-21

2) Hebrews 12:5-7, 11-13

3) Luke 13:22-30

22nd Sunday

1) Sirach 3:17-18, 20, 28-29

2) Hebrews 12:18-19, 22-24a

3) Luke 14:1, 7-14

23rd Sunday

1) Wisdom 9:13-18b

2) Philemon 1:9b-10, 12-17

3) Luke 14:25-33

24th Sunday

1) Exodus 32:7-11, 13-14

2) 1 Timothy 1:12-17

3) Luke 15:1-32

25th Sunday

1) Amos 8:4-7

2) 1 Timothy 2:1-8

3) Luke 16:1-13

26th Sunday

1) Amos 6:1a, 4-7

2) 1 Timothy 6:11-16

3) Luke 16:19-31

27th Sunday

1) Habakkuk 1:2-3, 2:2-4

2) 2 Timothy 1:6-8, 13-14

3) Luke 17:5-10

28th Sunday

1) 2 Kings 5:14-17

2) 2 Timothy 2:8-13

3) Luke 17:11-19

29th Sunday

1) Exodus 17:8-13

2) 2 Timothy 3:14—4:2

3) Luke 18:1-8

30th Sunday

1) Sirach 35:12-14, 16-18

2) 2 Timothy 4:6-8, 16-18

3) Luke 18:9-14

31st Sunday

1) Wisdom 11:23—12:2

2) 2 Thessalonians 1:11—2:2

3) Luke 19:1-10

32nd Sunday

1) 2 Maccabees 7:1-2, 9-14

2) 2 Thessalonians 2:16—3:5

3) Luke 20:27-38

33rd Sunday

1) Malachi 3:19-20a

2) 2 Thessalonians 3:7-12

3) Luke 21:5-19

34th Sunday (Christ the King)

1) 2 Samuel 5:1-3

2) Colossians 1:12-20

3) Luke 23:35-43

Meet the Author and Presenters

Mark Hart, author and lead presenter, is a man on a mission: spreading the gospel. Affectionately known as the "Bible Geek," Mark serves as executive vice president for Life Teen International. He is a graduate of the University of Notre Dame, the author of seven books, and the author and presenter of *T3: The Teen Timeline* and *Encounter* Bible study programs from *The Great Adventure*. Mark's creative work on videos and written resources is known internationally.

Jackie Francois Angel is a Catholic recording artist and speaker who travels both nationally and internationally, leading retreats and conferences for youth and young adults. Her debut album, *Your Kingdom Is Glorious*, was released through OCP/SpiritandSong.com. Jackie and her husband, Bobby Angel, live in California with their infant daughter.

Fr. Joshua Johnson is a newly ordained priest in the Diocese of Baton Rouge. He has spoken at conferences for teenagers and adults, sharing his conversion experience and proclaiming a message of hope and restoration of the dignity of the human person.

Fr. Michael Schmitz serves as both the director of youth and young-adult ministry for the Diocese of Duluth and as the chaplain for Newman Catholic Campus Ministry at the University of Minnesota-Duluth in Duluth, Minnesota. He also travels nationally and internationally giving talks and leading retreats and conferences.

Chris Stefanick is a co-author and lead presenter for *Chosen*. Chris has served at a parish in the East Los Angeles area and as director of youth and young-adult ministry for the Archdiocese of Denver. He is the founder and president of Real Life Catholic, a nonprofit organization dedicated to re-engaging a generation. Chris is a syndicated columnist, has authored or co-authored several books, and is a regular on Catholic TV and radio.

Ike Ndolo was born in Missouri to Nigerian parents and grew up in a home that rang with hymns sung by his mother. His love of music and talent as a musician and worship leader has been encouraged by his mentors, Tom Booth and Matt Maher. Ike leads worship every Sunday at his church in Tempe, Arizona, and he travels the country leading others to Christ. Ike's second album *Rivers* was released in 2012.

Acknowledgments

With gratitude to the many souls who shared Christ's truth with me—especially when I did not want to hear it, during my teenage years—too many to list but to whom I'm (literally) eternally grateful.

To my best friend and wife, Melanie, who endured many early morning and late night writing sessions beside me and sacrificed so much during my extra trips and additional calls ... your constant support and insight always make me better. I love you more than you can fathom.

To my children ... I hope you will one day understand why Daddy did the things he did and that through my ongoing (though failed) attempts at unconditional, love you will come to believe in the Father's perfect love.

To Fr. Dan Beeman ... you are a gift to me, to my family, and to Christ's Church. Thank you for your daily "yes" and for being such a great example of the joy, majesty, and humility of the priesthood.

To Fr. Bob Schreiner, Fr. John Muir, and Fr. John Parks, whose conversations, priestly presence, and insights helped shape this resource into the beautiful work that it became.

To Randy Raus and the staff, missionaries, board, priests, youth ministers, and core members of Life Teen around the world: You are the holiest and most talented souls a person could ever serve beside, thank you for who you are and all you do for the Lord, his teens, and his Church!

To Chris Cope and Steve Motyl, whose willingness to take risks and "put out into the deep" will still be felt long after we've been called home. Thank you for taking Catholic resources to the next level.

To Philip Braun, who only knows how to shoot beautifully: Thanks for always going the extra mile, even in the twelfth hour.

To Nick DeRose, the unsung hero who was forced to listen to my voice endlessly during video editing ... some use a brush, others a chisel, but every click from your hands is a work of art, brother.

To the writers, editors, and designers, for putting their gifts at the service of the Lord and his Church: Patrick McCabe, Mike Flickinger, Lora Brecker, Stella Ziegler, and Mike Fontecchio.

To all of our presenters, for sharing the gift that they are with young people: Fr. Michael Schmitz, Chris Stefanick, Fr. Josh Johnson, and Jackie Francios-Angel,

To Ike Ndolo, Emily Wilson and the band ... you always help my heart open to the Lord in new ways when we worship together.

And finally, to Matthew Pinto—the "King of Analogies"—whose tireless work for the kingdom and urgency to share the gospel in new ways is unrivaled. Thank you for leading the way with Ascension Press, smashing the jar and pouring out the precious oil so that our King would be glorified.

What an honor it is to toil in the vineyard beside all of you. May we never weary, nor lose perspective of what an inestimable privilege it is to preach and serve in his Name.

All for her Son!

Mark Hart